Natural Wonders of the British Isles

A voyage of discovery

by

Robert Morrow

Published 2022 by Morrow Associates

Contents

Introduction

If this title seems a little pretentious, I can only say, in my defence, that it was the title of the second Noble Caledonia cruise to be embarked upon after the partial easing of the Covid-19 lockdown in 2021. My original booking was for "Springtime in the Hebrides", departing from and returning to Oban, but the Scottish Government's rules suddenly precluded any landings on Scottish soil and the cruise had to be rerouted.

Map produced by Ian Bullock

Day 1: Joining the MS Island Sky

My adventure started when Russ dropped me off at Darlington station to catch the 9:17 TransPennine Express to Liverpool Lime Street. The first-class carriage was almost empty; naturally, the only other occupants, a woman with her young child, occupied my reserved seat. It would have been churlish to complain.

It was an uneventful, if slowish, journey. A cup of coffee would have been nice, but nothing was on offer!

I arrived at Lime Street Station at noon and was met by charming representatives of Noble Caledonia and escorted to the waiting coach. Being first, I was able to take a front seat. About ten others joined and we were treated to a brief guided historical tour as we headed to the Royal Dock where our ship awaited us.

MS Island Sky, with its sister ship, MS Hebridean Sky, is the largest ship in the small Noble Caledonia fleet. Described as "two of the finest small ships in the world", they are not large – only 300 feet long and 50 feet in beam, weighing in at 4,200 tons and with fifty-nine double cabins for a maximum of one hundred and eighteen guests.

After being tested to ensure that we were free of Covid-19, we passed through security and joined the ship, where champagne and afternoon tea/coffee awaited us. I chatted to Judith and David from Norfolk. They have cruised with Noble Caledonia before. This, I was to find, seemed to be true of most of the passengers. They were slightly dismissive when they asked me which deck I was on. "We don't think a balcony matters, we're quite happy with a porthole. We'll spend so little time in the cabin." Ah, well, time would tell.

My cabin steward, Pranata, was waiting to greet me and show me to my cabin as I walked onto the Erikson deck, one below the top!

The deluxe cabin with private balcony, to which I had upgraded a few days earlier, was not a disappointment! At twenty-five square yards, with a large double bed, well-appointed toilet/shower, and a walk-in wardrobe with forty decent, wooden coat-hangers – yes, I counted them! – it really merited its deluxe description.

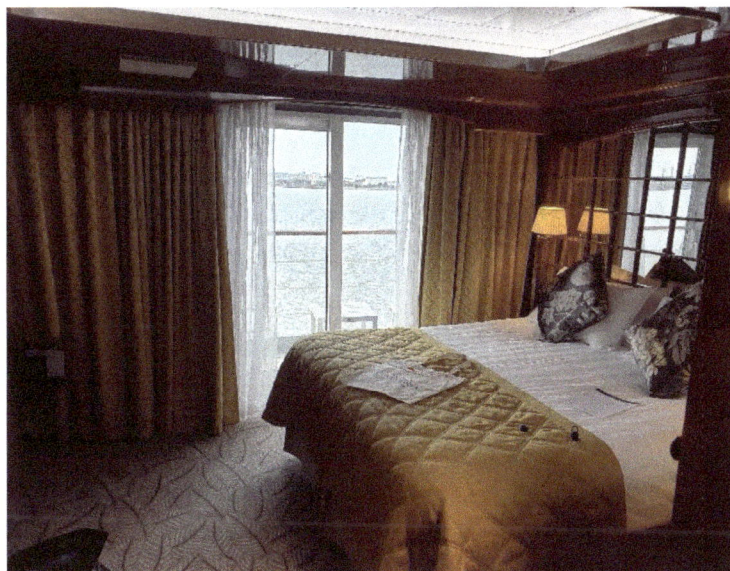

From the deck of the MS Island Sky, we had excellent views of the Three Graces – from centre to right, the Royal Liver Building, the Cunard Building, and the Port of Liverpool Building. These buildings are part of what was, until recently, a UNESCO-designated World Heritage Maritime Mercantile City, a status lost because of recent developments, including the new Everton Football Club stadium.

The Royal Liver Building was opened in 1911, home of the Royal Liver Assurance group. One of the first buildings in the world to be built using reinforced concrete, it is 322 feet tall to the top of the spires. It is one of the most recognisable landmarks in the city of Liverpool and is home to the two fabled Liver Birds that watch over the city and the sea. Legend has it that if these two birds were to fly away, then the city would cease to exist.

The Cunard Building was opened in 1917. Its style is a mix of Italian Renaissance and Greek Revival. The building is noted for the ornate sculptures that adorn its sides. Until the 1960s, it was the headquarters of the Cunard Line, and was home to Cunard's passenger facilities for trans-Atlantic journeys departing from Liverpool. It is located diagonally across the Strand from Albion House, the former headquarters of the White Star Line, owners of the ill-fated Titanic, of which more anon.

Formerly the Mersey Docks and Harbour Board Offices and more commonly known as the Dock Office, the Port of Liverpool Building was constructed between 1904 and 1907, with a reinforced concrete frame clad in Portland Stone. In Edwardian Baroque style, it is noted for the large dome that sits atop it.

At 16:30, we had the mandatory SOLAS (Safety of Lives at Sea) drill and at 17:45, to the accompaniment of broadcast Beatles music from the dock, we "set sail" for Rathlin Island. The lounge was not crowded. At least partly as a result of Covid-19 restrictions, there were only forty-nine passengers rather than the one hundred and eighteen possible. (I was advised that the crew totalled about sixty! What a good ratio!)

At 18:45, it was time for a general introduction and the compulsory Zodiac safety briefing. I was left feeling slightly daunted by the prospect of clambering aboard a rubber dingy.

Dinner followed shortly afterwards. The food was excellent, wine flowed liberally, and the staff, as they were everywhere on board, were polite and helpful. I had opted for a table alone rather than lumber, and be lumbered with, another two or three people for the first four days of fixed seating, after which some freedom would be permitted. It gave me the opportunity to observe and overhear my fellow passengers!

Most tables were for four people, maximum of two households. The travellers were nearly all couples, in the old-fashioned sense, with a few same-gender pairs (not necessary "couples") and one mother-and-daughter. There was only one table-for-one – mine!

I estimated the average age to be about seventy. There was a handful of younger – but not young – people but the majority were at least in their seventies. However, this was no SAGA cruise! They were old but definitely not frail - not one of them, or more properly, us - indicated any reluctance to volunteer for the Zodiac trips round Rathlin Island in the morning.

My impression was that, by and large, my fellow travellers were not necessarily rich but, on the whole, "comfortably off".

At the foot of the dessert menu was an invitation to "join our musician Rosario Ronallo in the Club Bar on deck 4 and see our special selection of After Dinner Drinks". I did so and, for quite some time, I was the lone audience! The music was pleasant and of an age-appropriate vintage – *Yesterday, A Nightingale Sang in Berkeley, Smoke Gets in Your Eyes* and so on. And smoke did, just for a moment, when I recalled the words "here comes Mary, hair of gold and lips like cherries" as he played *Green, Green Grass of Home*.

I bought a drink for "Ros" and, over the next hour or so, I enjoyed three Cosmopolitans. Two couples came and went quite quickly, sitting in the library - presumably to escape the piano music - and another two couples sat and chatted for a while. I heard one gentleman observe that he had quite a selection of whiskies at home – but he seemed to be drinking water! Already. any idea I might have had that this was going to be a riotous social event had quickly evaporated!

Ros sat and chatted to me for a little while. He is Canadian of Italian extraction and has been working on cruise ships for many years. Complaining of an upset stomach, he left his Cosmopolitan almost untouched and suddenly went off.

I went to bed!

Day 2: Rathlin Island and the Giant's Causeway.

I woke before my 6:45 alarm and was able to view the sun rise over the "*mist rolling in from the sea*" on the Mull of Kintyre, as Sir Paul McCartney once wrote.

By breakfast time, we had anchored at the southern end of Rathlin Island, just off the northeast coast of Antrim, and only 15 miles from Kintyre. Roughly J-shaped, it measures about 4 miles from east to west, and 2½ miles from north to south. The only inhabited offshore island of Northern Ireland, it once had a population of over one thousand. There are now only about one hundred and fifty inhabitants, mainly congregated in the small settlement of Church Bay, but the population is growing once again.

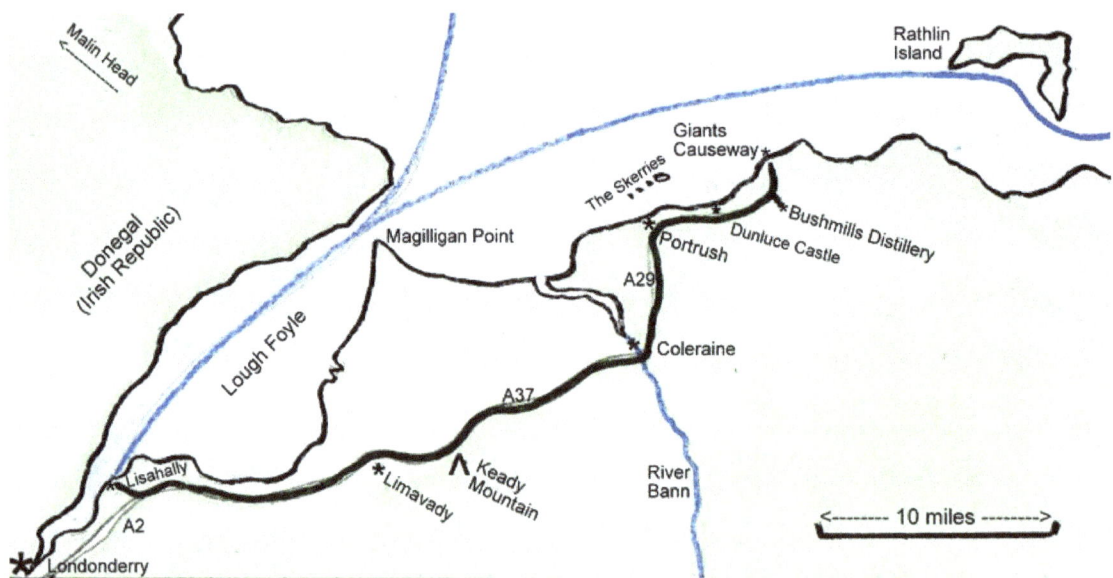

Volcanic in origin, the island is plateau-like, as a result of glaciation.

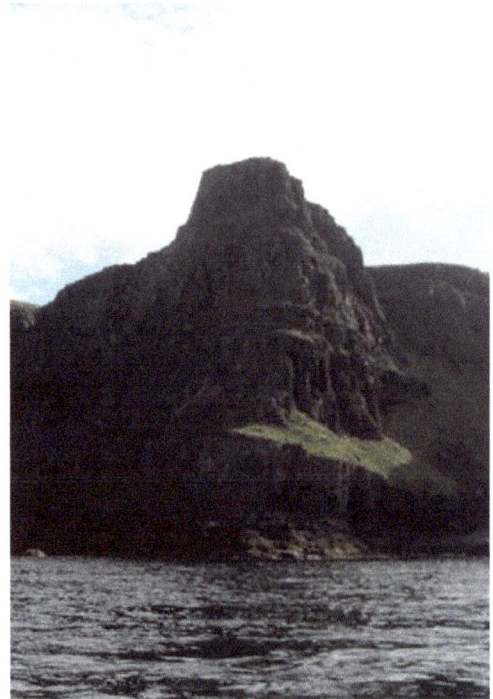

The highest point, *Slieveard*, is only 440 feet above sea level. Nevertheless, the 230-foot sea cliffs are impressive and home to tens of thousands of seabirds – about thirty bird families in total. Northern Ireland's only breeding pair of choughs can, apparently, be seen during the summer months. We did not!

I was on the first Zodiac, piloted by historian and our guide-for-the-day, Phil Wickens. There were only six passengers on each, instead of the usual ten, because of Covid-19 restrictions. That was no bad thing as it gave us more freedom to turn around and observe! We motored around for over an hour, viewing a plethora of sea-birds – cormorants, guillemots, black guillemots, shags, razorbills, puffins, eider ducks and kittiwake, to name but a few – as well as both harbour and grey seals.

Guillemots

Razorbill

Common/Harbour seals

Next, we cruised westerly along the southern side of the island with a running commentary about the island's history, geology and the bird colonies at the western end.

Many famous figures from history are associated with the island. Thus: -

It is said that St Columba spent time here, on his way from Ireland to Iona.

King Robert the Bruce was inspired by the determined spider in a cave at Altacarra Head.

Marconi set up a wireless link between Rathlin Island (the most important point in Lloyd's chain of information on ships arriving from America or Canada) and Ballycastle. Marconi's assistant, George Kemp, sent and received signals on August 26th 1898, reporting twelve ships to Lloyd's, even though there was thick fog – the start of radio communications!

Sir Richard Branson's hot-air balloon crashed into the sea off Rathlin after his record-breaking trans-Atlantic flight from Maine, USA.

At 13:20, the pilot joined us to guide us into Lough Foyle, heading for Londonderry Port at Lisahally. We passed Magilligan Point, where we could see the sandy beach and the well-preserved Martello tower. Built around 1815, during the Napoleonic Wars, to guard against possible invasion, it is one of the most northerly of the seventy-four towers built all around the coasts of Ireland.

We hugged the western edge of the lough - that is, the Donegal/ Irish Republic side, at the northern end of which is Mallin Head, the northernmost point of the island of Ireland.

(Historical Note: The German U-boat fleet surrendered at Lisahally on 14th May 1945. After the first eight, other U-boats arrived over the next few weeks and eventually between forty and sixty were sunk at sea in Operation Deadlight.)

A lecture by Dr Susan Currie on the geology of the various locations we had visited and planned to visit, was extremely interesting. Unfortunately, I did not take notes but, later, I asked her if she could produce a one-page summary for us and she agreed. Unfortunately, I still have not seen it! Perhaps it was an unreasonable request.

The original plan had been to dock at Portrush but, at the last minute, the authorities there had changed their minds and we had to head, instead, for Lisahally at the mouth of the River Foyle, a few miles north of Londonderry and a lot further away than Portrush from the Giant's Causeway.

This change required an hour-long coach trip. We skirted round Limavady, passing Keady Hill (or Mountain, although it is only 1,106 feet high) at the northern end of the Sperrin Mountains. (Plumbridge, whence my Irish ancestors hail, is at the south-western end of this 'mountain' range.)

From there we bypassed Coleraine and headed towards the coast. As we passed the Royal Portrush Golf Course and the Skerries, our guide told tales of shipwrecks on the rocks, including the Girona, a galleass from the Spanish Armada, which was wrecked in a storm in 1588. Of the 1300 men on board the ship, just nine survived. The cannons from the ship were installed in the gatehouses of Dunluce Castle and the rest of the cargo sold, the funds being used to restore the castle.

A little further on, we passed a stretch of cretaceous chalk cliffs. Further east, the White Rocks abut the sea, where they demonstrate classic coastal landforms in chalk - cliff, shore platform, cave, arch, and sea stack. Unfortunately, we did not see those, but we did have time to stop, albeit briefly, for a photo opportunity at Dunluce Castle.

Dunluce Castle

The first castle at Dunluce was built in the 13th century, located on the edge of a basalt outcrop and surrounded by steep drops to the sea. It later became the home of the chief of the Clan MacDonnell of Antrim and the Clan MacDonald of Dunnyveg, second son of Good John of Islay, Lord of the Isles, 6th chief of Clan Donald in Scotland. It served as the seat of the Earl of Antrim until the impoverishment of the MacDonnells in 1690, following the Battle of the Boyne. After that, the castle deteriorated, and parts were scavenged to serve as materials for nearby buildings.

Lying adjacent to Dunluce Castle, although we could not see its remains, is the "lost town of Dunluce", which was razed to the ground in the Irish uprising of 1641. Built around 1608 by Randall MacDonnell, the first Earl of Antrim, it pre-dates the official Plantation of Ulster. It was an ill-advised development as there was no easy access to the sea for essential trade and communications.

The coach tour also gave our local guide time to claim that the Irish had a dislike for the Scots and their theft of the Irish inventions of golf and whisky – or, as he would have spelled it, whiskey. Inevitably, some banter ensued between us!

The National Trust had agreed to keep the Giant's Causeway visitors' centre open for us and we had guides to take each of our three groups down to the causeway.

This is a series of some 40,000 interlocking, eroded, polygonal basalt columns, formed some sixty million years ago by the slow cooling, under pressure, of a volcanic sill. Most of the columns are hexagonal, although there are also some with four, five, seven, eight (and possibly even nine) sides.

The tallest columns are about forty feet high, and the solidified lava in the cliffs is over ninety feet thick in places. The tops of some columns are domed, others are concave.

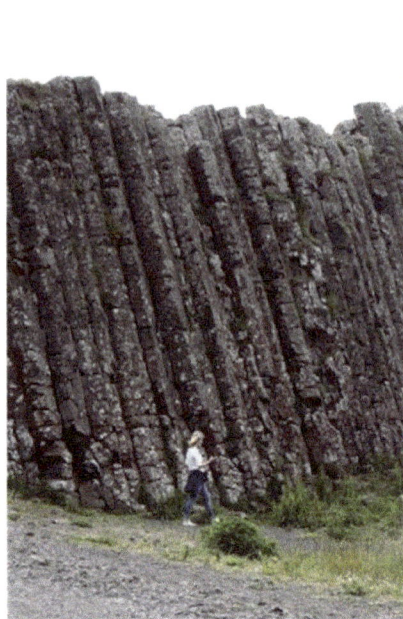

Other geological features in the area of the causeway are onion stones and red laterite.

As the eruptions which formed the Lower Basalts got less and less frequent, there was a longer dormant period (of at least a hundred thousand years). A warm and wet climate wore down the top of the basalt; plants grew and helped form a deep red soil. This appears as a thick red layer, called laterite, in the cliffs.

The basalt rock has been disintegrating to form rounded, spherical boulders that are sitting in a soft, brown, crumbly 'soil'.

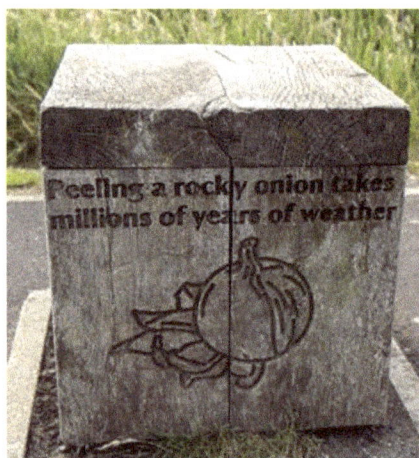

Peeling a rocky onion takes millions of years of weather

When the rocks expand in the sun's heat by day and then cool and contract at night, small pieces of rock fall off, forming a soft skin on the boulders so that they look like a thin layer of onion skin, hence the name "Onion Skin weathering".

Our guide was not only informative but also quite entertaining. Susan Curie was leader of our group and, having already informed us how the basalt columns were really formed, she could only roll her eyes in amusement at the tales of the Irish giant, Finn MacCool and his battle with the even-larger, Scottish giant, Benandonner, throwing stones and insults at each other.

As the story goes, on accepting the challenge to fight, Finn built the causeway so that the two giants could meet. Realising his foe was much bigger than he, Finn's wife disguised Finn as a baby and tucked him into a cradle. When Benandonner saw the size of the "baby", he reckoned that its father, Finn, must be a giant among giants and fled back to Scotland in fright, destroying the causeway behind him so that Finn would be unable to chase him down.

Across the sea, there are identical basalt columns (a part of the same ancient lava flow) at Fingal's Cave on the Scottish isle of Staffa, and no doubt this influenced the story's creation.

Amazingly, and pleasingly, we were all back on the coaches before the planned departure time. (This was to be a feature of all our trips – on not one occasion were we kept waiting for late arrivals. This was most definitely not a SAGA cruise!)

This early departure allowed us to pay a fleeting visit to the car park of the Bushmills distillery – and, of course, to allow our guide to make further, somewhat biased, comparisons between Irish and Scotch whisky. (At the end of the tour, I gave him a fiver and suggested he treat himself properly – to a dram of Highland Park or Glenmorangie. It was all taken in good part on both sides!)

13

After the only slightly disappointing meal that I was to experience – the halibut was bland to the point of tasteless, although the pudding, as ever, was delicious and the wine free-flowing - I eschewed the delights of the lounge and went straight to bed.

At some time after eleven o'clock, delayed by an incoming tanker, we left Lisahally and headed northwards.

Most of the Expedition Team – Michelle, Colin, Phoebe, Justin, Fiona, Phil and Kevin

(Missing are Brenda, Ian and Susan)

Day 3: Mingulay, St Kilda (at last) and the Flannan Isles

I was conscious, during the night, that the sea was not as calm as previously, although it could hardly have been described as "rough". A "rolling sea" is, I think, the correct term.

I rose a little after 6:30, just in time to see, through the light morning mist, the islands of Mingulay and Berneray to starboard, south of Barra and still seventy miles from St Kilda. Our visit here would have to wait another two days.

We received an update on the itinerary by expedition leader, Colin Munro. Iona, originally a scheduled visit, had then become a "maybe for Zodiacs" but was now a "no". Staffa remained a "maybe". The Isle of Man, not on the original itinerary, appeared on the revised list, then on the "maybe" list, but now not on the list at all. Its replacement, Belfast, had now gone off the list, and the hope was that Larne would be added in its place. English destinations remain unchanged. Oh! The joy of Covid-19!

Just after noon, a minke whale was spotted, to great general excitement. It seemed to be alone in a vast expanse of ocean.

At the very end of an interesting talk, "Of birds and men. The St Kilda story" by ornithologist Ian Bullock, it was announced that St Kilda had hove into view.

We had made it, at last! The sea was calm, the sun shining in a clear, blue sky. For what more could anyone ask? (Apart from being allowed to land!)

St Kilda was the destination I had most craved. If this had been deleted from the list, then the whole trip would have been, in my mind, an abject failure. Ever since I had heard of and then read about the abandonment of the islands by the thirty remaining residents in 1930, it had been a journey I wanted to make.

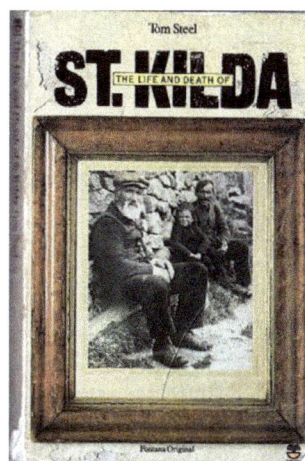

The story of the final desertion of St Kilda is so well known that I do not intend to repeat it here – but I do recommend Tom Steel's 1975 publication, "The Life and Death of St. Kilda", lent to me for pre-cruise reading by my good friend, Ross.

The St Kilda archipelago lies about forty miles from the nearest land, Lewis and Harris. The main island, Hirta, measures just over two miles from east to west and two miles from north to south. It has an area of just under three square miles. Although the island slopes gently down to the sea at Glen Bay (at the western end of the north coast), the rocks there go straight into the sea at a shallow angle.

And so, the only real landing place is in the shelter of Village Bay on the southeast side of the island. Our ship anchored there and from it we could see the ruined cottages and the stone *cleits* in which food – mainly seabirds - was dried and stored.

There are new buildings as well, nowadays, because of the presence of an army unit and, in summer, RSPB volunteers.

Covid-19 regulations prohibited our landing on this island and, indeed, on any Scottish soil but despite the Scottish government's insistence that we could not land, there were a few smaller boats in the bay. Who checked where they came from and the status of their vaccinations? Rhetorical question.

Over lunch, the expedition crew "tested the water" and shortly after two o'clock I joined the first Zodiac excursion, with Expedition Leader, Colin Munro. We explored the cliffs of the island of Dun (to the south-east of Hirta), viewing the plethora of birdlife and a few inquisitive seals.

According to Colin, there is a one-hundred-yard-long tunnel, accessible only at very low tide, from one side of Dun to the other. We did not venture to find it but contented ourselves with passing through one of the arches!

Once we had steered our way through to the other side of the island, we were out of the protection of Dun and Hirta and the sea became just a little rougher.

On St Kilda, there are estimated to be 300,000 pairs of puffins (50% of the entire UK population), 60,000 pairs of gannets, 40,000 pairs of fulmars, 20,000 pairs of guillemots, 10,000 pairs of kittiwakes, plus Manx shearwaters, storm petrels, Leach's petrels and great skuas.

Kittiwake

A sea-full of puffins!

 Once all were safely back on board, the MS Island Sky began a tour around the west of Hirta. Hirta boasts the highest sea cliffs in the British Isles – as much as 1,400 fet..

Soay is separated from Hirta by the 500-yard-wide Sound of Soay. The island covers about 240 acres and reaches a height of 1,240 feet, the cliffs rising sheer out of the sea.

There are no Soay sheep left on Soay but, apparently, there are some on Boreray. (I did not see any sign of them but, a few days later, we were fortunate to see some of the small herd that is maintained on Lundy, some six hundred miles to the south.)

Two sea stacks, *Stac Shoaigh* ("Shovel Stack", 200 feet), and *Stac Biorach*, ("Sharp Stack", 240 feet), lie between Hirta and Soay. *Stac Biorach* was the main breeding ground for the guillemots that were collected by the islanders. It was nicknamed "Thumb Stack" because the only firm holds available on the sheer face were the size of a thumb. It was a proof of manhood for a young man to stand on top of the stack, on one leg, holding the other foot in his hand.

We passed around Soay and out towards Boreray.

We threaded our way between *Stac Lee* (564 feet, left) and *Stac an Armin* ("Stack of the soldier/warrior", 643 feet, above) to view and listen to the second largest gannet colony in Britain. (The Bass Rock, with 75,000 breeding pairs, is the largest.)

One gannet amongst thousands!

During its long history of inhabitation, the men (and boys) of Hirta visited the stacks annually to collect eggs and birds to sustain them through the winter. It was not unusual for them to stay for days and, occasionally, longer if conditions deteriorated. The longest recorded period anyone ever spent on the stack was about nine months. Three men and eight boys were marooned on the 643-foot *Stac an Armin* from about 15th August 1727 until 13th May 1728. Hirta had suffered a smallpox outbreak while the eleven were on the stack, and the islanders were unable to man a boat to retrieve them until the next year. It is truly impossible to imagine how they survived.

The last great auk seen in Britain was caught and killed on *Stac an Armin* in July, 1840.

Rounding Boreray, we headed northeast towards the north of Lewis.

Earlier in the day, while the sun shone on Hirta, a cloud had formed over Boreray. By the time of our departure, a heavy shroud of mist had descended over the archipelago, and the sea had become a little rougher, providing just a slightly better idea of life on St Kilda than that suggested by the benign conditions that had greeted our arrival.

We were invited for Welcome Drinks and a briefing before the Welcome Dinner. I was surprised, and a little disappointed, to find that there were no more than five men wearing jackets and only one tie was in evidence – mine! The captain did not appear – apparently, he had been up since six o'clock, poor wee soul.

(As an aside, I have to say that I found my fellow passengers a little less than welcoming – i.e. no-one spoke to me. No doubt, however, I had sent an "I-want-to-be-alone" message by opting for a mealtime table-for-one. I was delighted, therefore, when the cruise director, Brenda McLoughlin, asked if she would like one of the crew members to join me for dinner in future. Thank you, Brenda.)

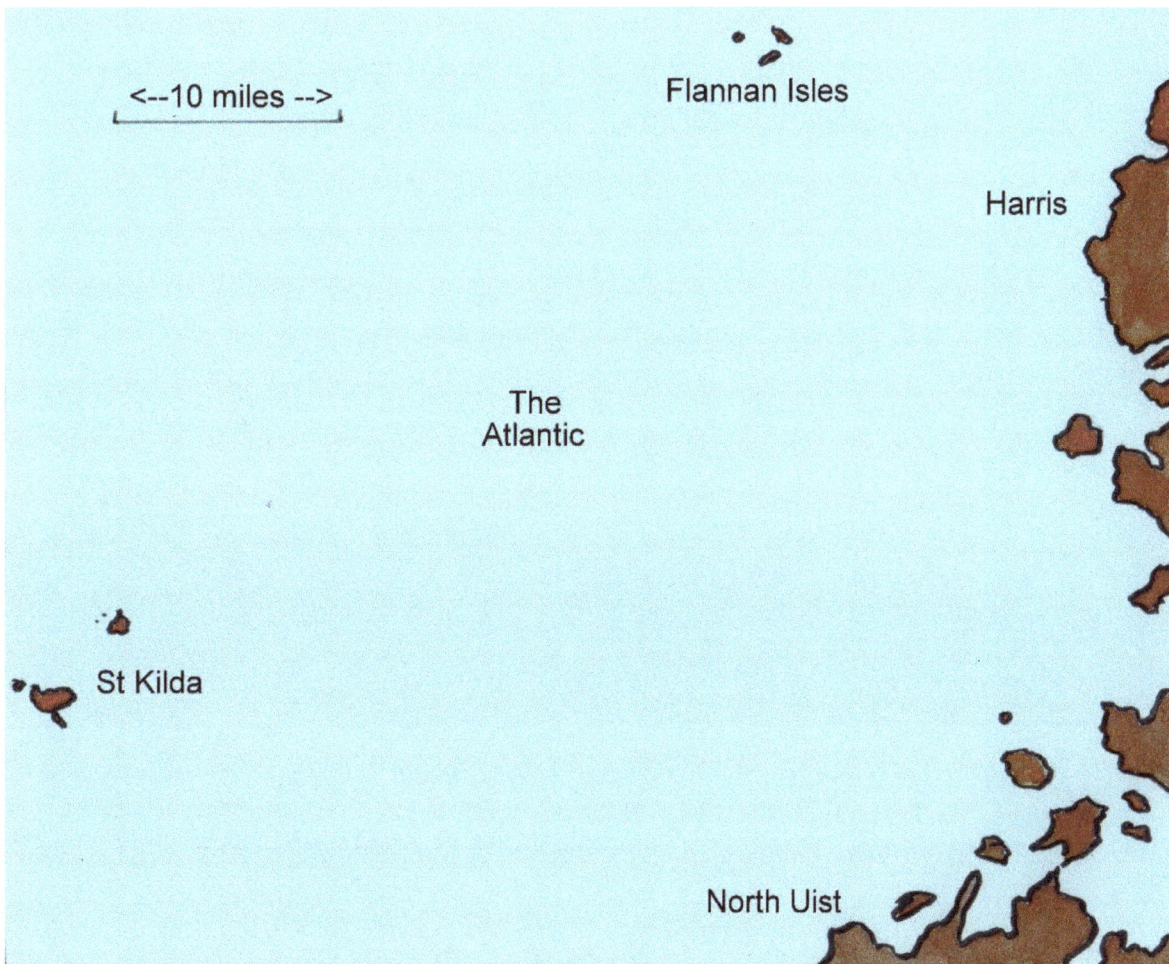

At 21:07, I noticed on the cabin monitor map that we were passing the Flannan Isles. Through the mist, I was able to glimpse and photograph this low-lying outcrop, twenty-one miles west of Aird Uig on Lewis and about half-way between the north of Lewis and St Kilda. My first thought was that these were Scottish islands of which I had never even heard!

However, on checking my guidebook, I was reminded of the tale of the three lighthouse-keepers who disappeared in mysterious circumstances in 1900, leaving an untouched meal at the table and only two missing oilskins. No satisfactory explanation of their disappearance has ever been provided.

As Wilfrid Wilson Gibson wrote in his poem about the events on the island: -

> *Though three men dwell on Flannan Isle*
> *To keep the lamp alight,*
> *As we steer'd under the lee, we caught*
> *No glimmer through the night.*

The lighthouse was not automated until 1971. And so, for seventy years, the lighthouse keepers who manned the light after that disappearance must often have wondered, even feared for, what had happened to their colleagues.

Day 4: The Shiant Isles and Loch Torridon

I caught my first glimpse of the Shiants through the mist as we approached at seven am. They did not look particularly enchanting, as their Gaelic name suggests they should.

In The Minch, just five miles off the east coast of Lewis, the three main Shiant islands - *Garbh Eilean* ("rough island") and *Eilean an Taighe* ("house island"), which are joined by a narrow isthmus, and *Eilean Mhuire* ("island of the Virgin Mary") to the east - cover a total of 350 acres.

The islands were inhabited, on and off, for thousands of years until the early twentieth century. At the end, only a shepherd, his wife and two allegedly beautiful daughters were left. One day, when the wife was collecting birds and eggs, the rope by which her husband was holding her broke, and she plunged into the sea. The birds tucked into her belt were sufficiently buoyant to stop her from sinking – and so she was swept out beyond safety by the strong currents.

The islands are now occupied solely by birds and a few sheep, although there is reportedly a bothy somewhere. It is without food. When we visited, some intrepid travellers had pulled their rubber boat onto the shingle bank between *Garbh Eilean* and *Eilean an Taighe*. It was unclear whether or not they intended to stay.

Sir Compton Mackenzie, he of Barra and *Whisky Galore* fame, bought the islands in 1935 then resold them to the publisher Nigel Nicholson, in whose family ownership still remains.

With naturalist Justin Anderson at the helm of our Zodiac, we set off to watch the multitude of seabirds, amidst cries from my fellow passengers of "black guillemot", "oyster catcher", "lesser black-backed gull" and so on, and from fellow passenger Brian, as we entered a collapsed cave, "rock pipit". No-one else saw the rock pipit - but who am I to doubt an expert?

To put "multitude" into context, best estimates are that there are 15-18,000 guillemots, 8-11,000 razorbills, 4-6,000 fulmars, 2,000 kittiwakes, 1,500 shags and – wait for it - 240,000 puffins (one-eighth of the UK total and two percent of the world population).

Young cormorant with attentive parents (above).

Guillemot surrounded by razorbills (left).

If I never see another puffin in my life, however, it will be too soon! (I can hardly wait for Skomer and Lundy!) They are lovely little birds, of course, but they seemed to be absolutely everywhere.

A sad sighting, however, was of a great skua, pecking away at a dead puffin in the water; no doubt it had been a victim of a skua attack, a very frequent occurrence.

At one point, Justin thought he had seen a sea eagle perched on the edge of a sea cliff, some two hundred feet above us. Sadly, it turned out to be a raven – a good sighting in its own right but just a little disappointing!

We stopped for a while to watch a number of grey seals pop up their heads to watch us before disappearing and then reappearing in another spot.

The strait between the Island of Lewis and the Shiant Isles was known in the 19th century as the "Stream of the Blue Men" because it was said to be inhabited by a strange group of creatures. The Blue Men of the Minch, also known as Storm Kelpies, were said to occasionally prey on sailors making the crossing, demanding that they recite a particular poem (in Gaelic?) or they would seize or capsize the boat.

During our one-and-a-bit-hour Zodiac adventure around the Shiants, I was able to find out from his friend, Graham, that the afore-mentioned Brian is an award-winning (amateur) photographer - the "medium" lens he had with him was about two-feet long! - and a fine portrait painter to boot. Graham reckoned that Brian's lenses cost more than his, Graham's, car. Graham (and probably Brian, although Brian himself seemed uncertain) had already been to the Shiants. He had also been to Antarctica (twice), the Falklands (twice) South Georgia, the Galapagos – "you don't need a dry suit to dive there" – Indonesia, Mexico and many, many places that I simply cannot remember. Brian had been something quite high-powered in his career whereas Graham, he himself claimed, had been "just a simple retailer". Nevertheless, he had been able to retire at fifty-one, over twenty years ago. (In truth, the process of extracting all this information was quite simple – I just had to sit quietly and listen to Graham. Meanwhile, Brian said very little.)

Just before eleven o'clock, the anchor was hauled up and we headed south-east towards Loch Torridon. Shortly afterwards, we were called to the lounge for our fourth-day lateral flow test for Covid-19 by our on-board medical staff. Thankfully, all tests proved negative!

At around noon, a minke whale crossed in front of the ship, which veered through one hundred and eighty degrees to try to follow it. It was a vain, but noble, attempt and a measure of the lengths to which the ship's company will go in pursuit of views of nature for the passengers.

Brenda again joined me for lunch.

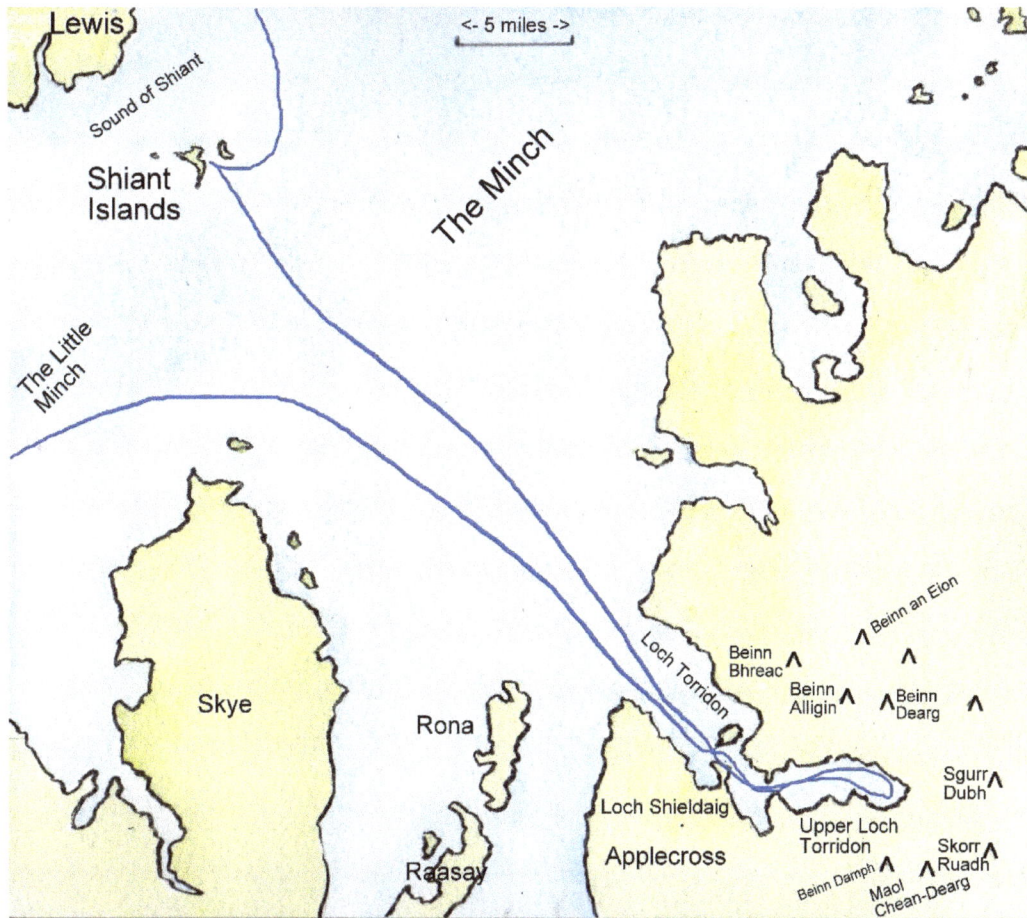

We entered Lower Loch Torridon at about 14:30 with the sun shining in a blue sky. There were claims by some to have seen one or more sea eagles over the Applecross peninsula, to our starboard (southern) side. but they were certainly beyond the capability of my binoculars. (One of my fellow Zodiac-sailors had remarked previously that he had bought his binoculars with the money that he had saved by not having a holiday last year. Obviously, they were a bit more expensive than those that I then secreted inside my coat!)

The captain threaded his way through the narrow gaps and over the glacial moraines between Lower Loch Torridon and Loch Shieldaig and between Loch Shieldaig and Upper Loch Torridon – an impressive if slightly worrying manoeuvre. (Apparently, he removes his shoes and socks to better feel the ship's behaviour at times like these.)

The various peaks and rock formations (gneiss, Torridon sandstone and quartzite) were pointed out to us as we traversed the thirteen miles into the loch.

In the sunshine, the views were very much better than those that I had "enjoyed" when I passed by, by car, less than one year earlier.

We were also given an explanation for the abundance of places in Scotland called Tarbert or similar. A tarbert is a low shingle bank joining two pieces of land. If a Viking was able to drag his long boat from the water on one side to the water on the other side, he could claim as his own that land surrounded by the sea and the tarbert. (Magnus Barefoot claimed the whole peninsula of Kintyre in this way, after Malcolm Canmore said that he could have whatever islands he could circumnavigate.)

The captain executed a tight turn at the head of the loch and we were soon heading back, through the narrows, to the mouth of the loch and the open sea. This was an unexpected and thoroughly enjoyable episode.

We passed Rona Island, at the northern end of Raasay Isle, beyond the point that I had reached by car a year earlier. The lighthouse was clearly visible.

Behind and to the west of Rona/Raasay, Skye was partially swathed in cloud although the "Far Cuillins" were just discernible in the distance.

By now, it was almost five o'clock and getting a little chillier. One of the great benefits of a private balcony now manifest itself – I could nip in and out as the scenery changed and invited inspection but then retreat quickly to the warmth of my boudoir!

An announcement to the effect that, because of a very poor signal, the crew had been unable to screen the Euro 2020 round-of-sixteen match between England and Germany, no doubt raised groans amongst the majority of passengers, but I did not hear them. In the event, England saw off the opposition with a fine 2-0 win.

As we turned southwards into The Little Minch, the stretch of water between Skye and the Uists, we received our normal recap and briefing, and a few tales and talks from the expedition crew.

I had a thoroughly enjoyable dinner with Susan Currie – the food was good as usual but, even better, the conversation was fun and stimulating as she recounted some of her experiences in the oil industry. She also gave me some ideas for things to do during my forthcoming visit to Aberdeen, where she had lived for twenty-five years.

Day 5: Staffa, the Treshnish Isles, and Mingulay

I rose very early, just as the ship anchored a little north of Iona and, it seemed, almost within touching distance of Staffa. The sea was like a millpond, the sun rising above the mists that hung over Mull.

I watched as the expedition crew set out on their exploratory trip towards Staffa.

Despite my, consequently unnecessary, early rise, I had decided not to go on the Zodiac trip to Staffa, not so much because "I've done that before" but because I feared it would be anticlimactic compared to last year's actual landing on the island and walking into Fingal's Cave. Perhaps it was a mistake – but at least I did avoid any disappointment.

Instead, I enjoyed the surrounding views of Mull, Iona and the Treshnish Islands and the sight of the Zodiacs plying their way to-and-fro. I also had the opportunity to chat to a couple of the crew members.

The name Staffa is derived from the Viking for "Island of Pillars".

It is clear just from looking at it, that Staffa and the Giant's Causeway are connected, albeit at a distance of some 82 miles. Known as the Collonade (sic!), the columns of basalt beneath the upper layer of jumbled and fractured columns and volcanic debris are even more pronounced here than in Ireland. And, of course, the Scottish version of the battle of giants may differ somewhat from the Irish one!

The cave became known as Fingal's Cave after the eponymous hero of an epic poem by 18th century Scottish poet-historian James Macpherson.

The island is now uninhabited but there are signs of settlements from bygone days.

Staffa became popular as a tourist destination after Turner painted it, and William Wordsworth, John Keats, Lord Tennyson, Jules Verne and Queen Victoria all visited the cave. Wordsworth penned a poem and Mendelssohn composed his evocative Hebridean Overture. The island is now owned and protected by the National Trust for Scotland.

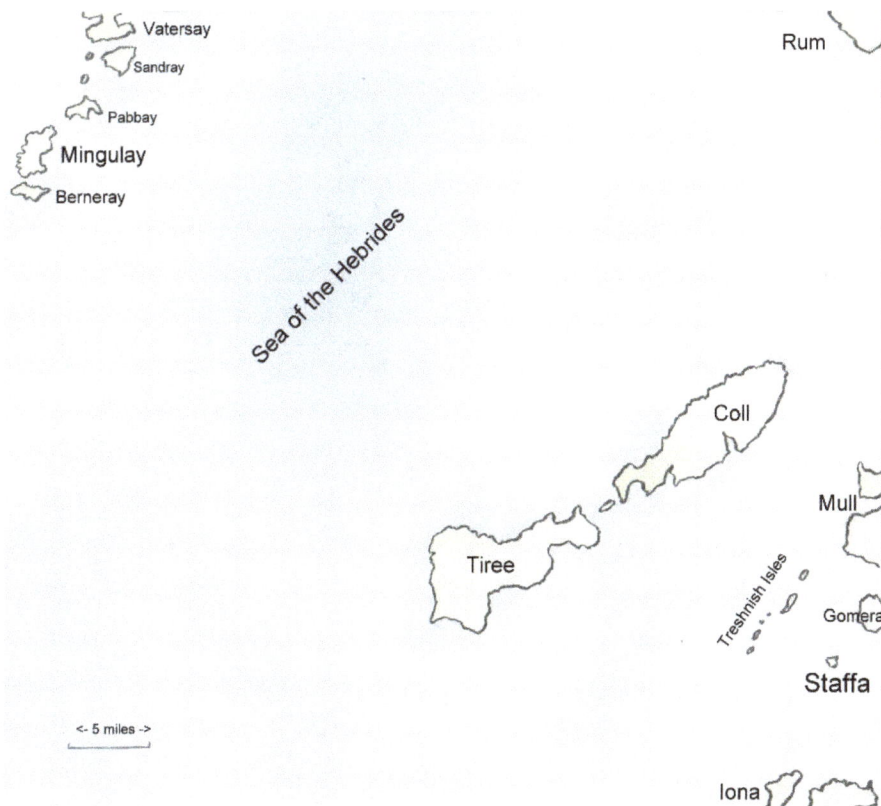

After our visit, we headed back northwards, passing, on our port side, the Treshnish Isles, an archipelago of volcanic isles no more than a couple of miles in width. I was a little disappointed that we did not have time to explore them. Lunga, the largest of them, is a nesting place for thousands of seabirds. The distinctive shape of *Bac Mor* lends it its nickname, "The Dutchman's Cap". Like so many of the small Hebridean islands, these islands were once inhabited – there are ruined castles on two of them – but not since 1715.

Rounding the northern tip of Coll, we steered almost due west across the Little Minch towards Mingulay. The sea was calm, but a light sea fret made for poor visibility – not that there is much to see other than low-lying Coll receding into the distance - and a chillier feeling on deck then the twelve-degree temperature suggested.

My prior knowledge of Mingulay was entirely based on the words of the Mingulay Boat Song and, accordingly, I should have liked to have seen "the sun set on Mingulay" but we would be long gone before that happened.

Mingulay's near neighbour, the smaller island of Berneray, is the southernmost island of the Outer Hebrides. Confusingly, Berneray is also the name for the northernmost of the five largest Uist islands.

After millennia of occupancy, with the population peaking at one hundred and sixty in the 1881 census, Mingulay was last inhabited in 1912, abandoned – like St Kilda – because of dwindling population and difficulty in getting food and medical supplies. Most of the residents headed for Vatersay, another rocky isle just to the south of Barra and about seven or eight miles north of Mingulay. The ruins of deserted houses still remain.

At the northern end of the island is Macphee's Hill. The story goes that Macphee, tax collector of McNeil of Barra, arrived on the island to find all the inhabitants had died of what he took to be plague. Hearing of this, his colleagues scarpered with the boat and Macphee was left on the island with the corpses. Each day, he climbed the hill to wave in vain to passing ships and it was some time before it was deemed safe to come and collect him.

The island was acquired by the NTS in 2000 and is now the home to seabirds, grasses, heather, bracken, and an assortment of wildflowers. Apparently, there is but one tree – a six-foot high poplar, perched on a cliff overlooking Mingulay Bay. Search as I did through my binoculars, I could not see it.

We dropped anchor near Mingulay Bay at about two o'clock. The bay lies on the east of the island, where it is sheltered by the hill behind from the prevailing westerly winds driving off the Atlantic. The nearest land to the west is over two thousand miles away at Nain, Labrador, Canada.

The bay has a fine sandy beach, beautiful to look at but probably not ideal for sun-bathing except on an exceptionally sunny day! There were kayaks already pulled up on the beach, a small yacht anchored in the bay, and a speedboat raced towards us until it veered away southwards.

After the expedition group returned from their exploratory venture, we were invited to board the Zodiacs. Although warned of a long trip, a significant swell between Berneray and Mingulay, and the possibility of getting cold and wet, I did not decline the invitation this time. Nor indeed, to my surprise, did the vast majority of passengers. One elderly woman on my Zodiac even turned up with bare feet in open-toed sandals. Ah, well, it takes all kinds!

On board again with Justin, we headed for the strait between the two islands. Justin pointed out what he thought were eagles – though he could not say whether white-tailed or golden – and I caught a glimpse through my binoculars before they disappeared from view.

On the western side, the sea was much calmer, thanks to the breeze being, unusually, easterly. We were able to view the Carnan cliffs, the most exposed sea cliffs in Britain, towering up to 800 feet, collapsed sea caves, plenty of sea birds, and a few seals.   **Grey seal** (below)

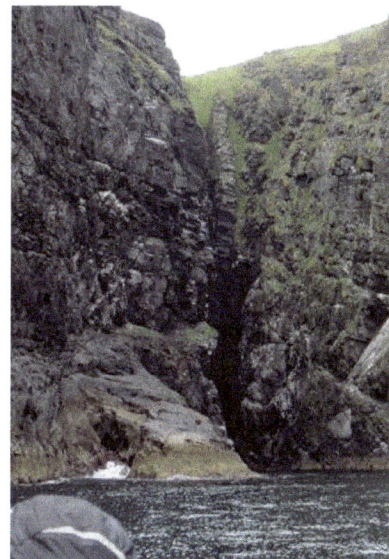

31

The highlight of this outing was probably the snoring of the Slumbering Giant, created by air being forced by the waves through a narrow slit in the rock. At first, the sound appeared to emanate from a cave above the slit and it was very easy to imagine a giant asleep inside.

We headed back towards the bay, but it was becoming quite choppy, so we did not approach the beach. It was also, as Justin pointed out, too rough for basking sharks, which are often seen in the bay. As we sped back, with Phil's boat ahead of us, it was clear that this was not an excursion for those prone to seasickness!

Altogether, this was a very enjoyable outing, with the usual hot drink (lemongrass tea this time) awaiting us on our return, and coffee and cake to follow!

By five o'clock, we were again underway, leaving the Outer Hebrides behind and heading south towards Larne.

A cry of "dolphins" off the port bow went up but they disappeared without my noticing them.

The normal evening briefing by Colin was followed by an excellent talk by Sue on geological time.

I had an enjoyable dinner with Brenda, discussing Noble Caledonia, her job, her book clubs, and her travels (and a bit about me, too, I confess). I gave her a copy of "Flying Visits" to peruse and she seemed happy to do so. Chef Tracie came across to chat; I complimented her on the meals. She was quite a character!

I considered, but then decided against, one wee dram before lights-out just after ten o'clock. It is hard work being on holiday!

Day 6: Larne, the Titanic Belfast Museum, and Glenarm Castle

I rose at 6:30 to find us edging our way slowly through fog into Larne harbour. It seemed entirely appropriate as we were heading for the Titanic Belfast Museum! Titanic is self-evidently not a "natural wonder" but, undoubtedly, it qualifies as a "Wonder of the British Isles".

Sue, our guide on the coach, was a former secondary schoolteacher. She was well-informed and very passionate about the environment and her country's history and achievements.

She pointed out the hedgerows that are protected by law (cannot be cut during March-August nor removed) and described the growth of the flax industry, initially a cottage industry, as being responsible for the creation of the docks and the inception of ship building in Northern Ireland. A statue on a roundabout enroute to Belfast celebrates the flax industry and its workers.

RMS Titanic is universally known, not for its size, its glamour, nor its cross-channel achievements, but as the unsinkable passenger liner that sank in the North Atlantic Ocean on 15th April 1912, after striking an iceberg during her maiden voyage from Southampton to New York City. Operated by the White Star Line, it was to be their star ship, bringing acclaim and great revenue to reward the investment. Instead, of the estimated 2,224 passengers and crew aboard, more than 1,500 died, making the sinking, at the time, one of the deadliest of a single ship and the deadliest peacetime sinking of a superliner or cruise ship to date.

Opened in 2012, exactly one hundred years after the disaster, the Titanic Belfast Museum is an excellent experience, a celebration of the design and building of what was then the world's largest ship rather than a memorial to its sinking, although the latter does not go unmarked.

As we moved around in our group bubble, the pace was quite fast, and I could have enjoyed more time on my own to appreciate all the displays and depictions. The museum attempted, very successfully, to recreate the scale of the operation and the sounds, the noise, of the shipyard as the giant ship was built – essentially by hand-power. I had not realised, but was delighted to see, that the rudder was manufactured by Darlington Forge.

There were displays, too, to demonstrate the space and the lavish furnishings (of the first-class accommodation) and a large selection of artefacts taken from the wreck.

Outside, there is a large wrought iron TITANIC sign, of the dimensions of the plates used to build the ship, and the pavement slabs show the route the ship had taken on its fateful voyage.

A hundred yards away, is the Nomadic, the smaller tender-ship that transferred passengers to Titanic at Cherbourg, whose docks could not accommodate the larger vessel. On the other side of the museum, although it is no longer a dock, the actual place where Titanic was built and launched is marked out.

Nearby, almost under Samson, one of two giant Harland & Wolf cranes, is the film set that was used for the scene in Game of Thrones, where the dragon destroys the castle. A large film studio is alongside.

Increasingly, filmmaking is becoming a major industry in Belfast.

Sadly, there is no longer any shipbuilding in Belfast nowadays – whilst there is still some maintenance and repair carried out, at Anvil Point, the last boat to be fully built in Belfast, slipped into the sea in 2003.

A short but very interesting coach-tour of the city centre followed our museum visit, including a drive past Belfast City Hall and, outside it, Sir Thomas Brock's fine white marble Titanic Memorial, displaying two nymphs holding aloft a drowning passenger..

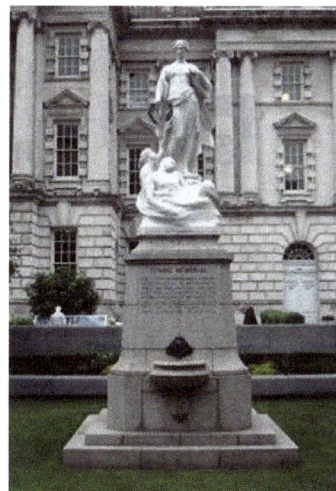

Sue also told us about Lilian Bland, an Anglo-Irish journalist and pioneer aviator who was the first woman in the British Isles, and perhaps even in the world, to design, build and fly an aeroplane. With an ironic reference to the time of her first attempt (May 1910) and her reservations about the airworthiness of her creation, she named it "Mayfly"!

Mayfly was first flown as a glider from Carnmoney Hill, to the west of Newtownabbey; the trials as a powered aircraft took place at the Deerpark in Randalstown, some twenty miles away.

Lilian did not pursue her aeronautical career. She gave the Mayfly airframe to a boy's gliding club, began running a car dealership in Belfast, married her lumberjack cousin and emigrated to Canada.

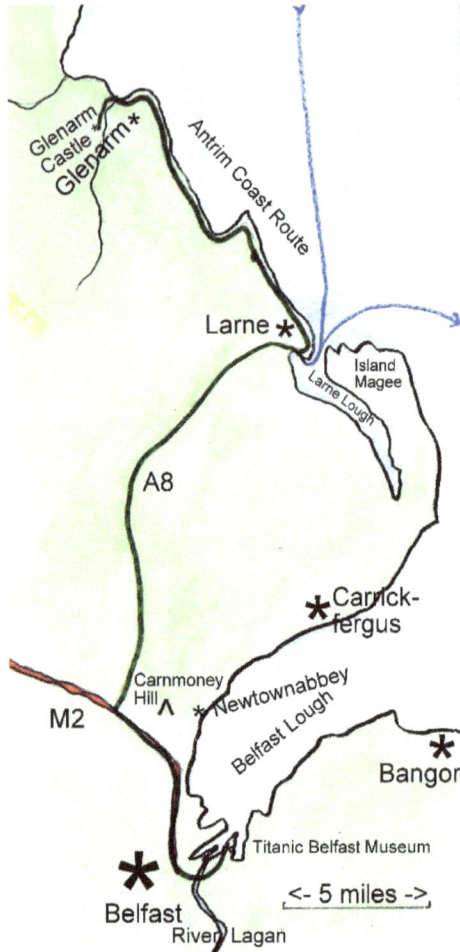

In the afternoon, we headed north through the town of Larne along the Antrim Coast Route, one of the most scenic routes in Ireland – "in the world", our guide, Christian, claimed, perhaps overegging it just a tad! After about ten miles or so, we turned up the valley of the Glenarm River and drove through the extensive farmlands of Glenarm Castle. The present castle was built in 1636 by, and is still owned by, the McDonnell family.

At the time of our visit, the castle was the family home of Randal, Viscount Dunluce, his wife Aurora, and their two children. Randal was son of Alexander McDonnell, 14th Earl of Antrim. The connection with Dunluce Castle, that we visited just three days earlier, apparently was not known (to our team) at the time this visit was arranged.

Sadly, since our visit, Lord Antrim died (on 21st July 2021), at the age of 86.

One of the earlier earls was an inveterate gambler who lost 300,000 acres (90%) of the land they owned along the north Antrim coast. This included Rathlin Island, lost on the turn of a playing card!

There is a historical connection – too convoluted to relate here – between the family and the Vane-Tempests of County Durham.

At the castle, we were welcomed by George, the butler, who conducted us on a guided tour of the entrance hall, drawing room, dining room and blue room. Afterwards we were given a tour of the walled garden – originally a kitchen garden but now an extensive tree, hedge, and floral garden.

George was an excellent and amusing guide. It is most unusual a) to be entertained by someone who not only knows the house in-and-out but actually knows the family intimately and b) to be invited to rest on the chairs in the furnished rooms.

Family photographs abounded and the whole house had a comfortable, lived-in feel – which is exactly what it was, a family home.

In the entrance hall, there were what can only be described as "strange" carvings created by the Viscount's mother. Other pieces she created were of a much more artistic quality - and especially a beautiful, life-size sculpture of the Madonna and Child in the walled garden, done when she was only sixteen.

Also in the entrance hallway, was a chest from the Girona, part of the Spanish Armada, whose sinking we had heard of on our way to the Giant's Causeway.

This was an excellent visit with unexpected connections to our earlier Northern Ireland outing.

Phil joined me for dinner, after which we repaired to The Club for several large Glenmorangies to round off the evening.

And why not?!

Day 7: Anglesey – Holyhead, Holy Isle, South Stack, and Plas Cadnant

Holyhead is the only large town on Holy Isle, which sits on the north-west corner of Anglesey, and is the largest town on Anglesey. It is believed that the name Anglesey does not refer to the Angles, as might be expected, but is derived from the Norse words "*Ongl's ey*", meaning Ongl's island. Ongl's identity must forever remain a mystery to me.

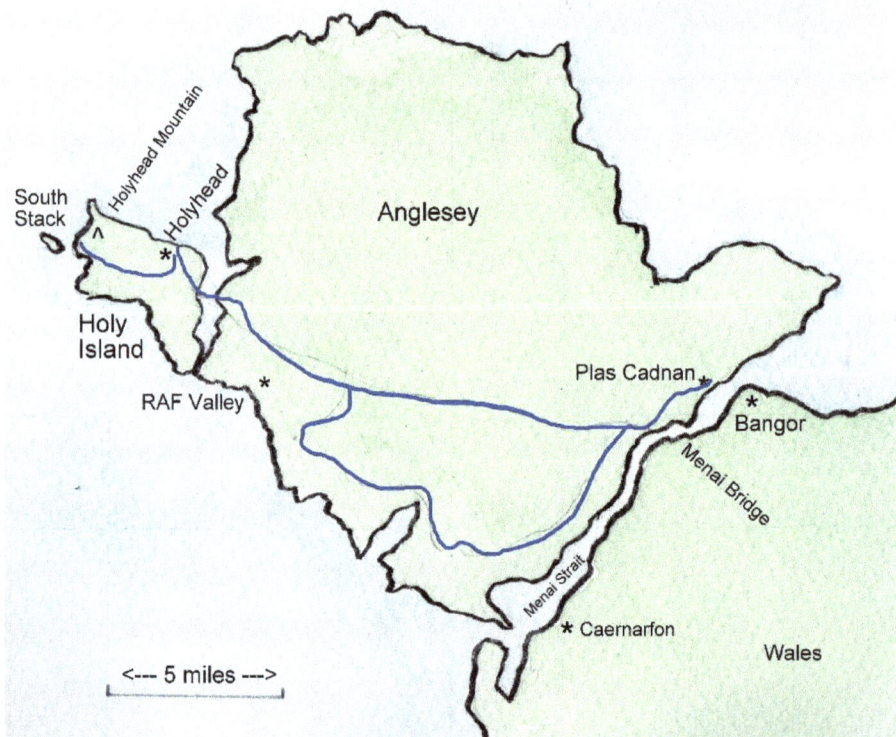

Our local guide, Amanda, explained that, until fairly recently, the major employers, apart from the docks, were the aluminium industry and the Wylfa Magnox nuclear power station. The power station has now been decommissioned and RTZ has "repositioned" to Argentina. There is talk of a new mini nuclear reactor being built but nothing has been confirmed. Meanwhile, Anglesey is endeavouring to brand itself as Energy Island, with the establishment of wind farms and wave/tidal power experiments. It is also endeavouring to become plastic-free, discouraging the use of plastic bottles, cutlery, etc.

A major Irish Sea port serving Ireland, Holyhead's 1.7-mile-long breakwater is the longest in the United Kingdom. It was built over twenty-eight years using seven million tons of locally quarried quartzite rock and was completed in 1873.

A significant feature of Holyhead harbour is the Celtic Gateway Bridge, designed to look like the tusks of a woolly mammoth. In 1864, a group of workmen came across what was subsequently identified as the teeth and jawbone of a female *Elephas Primigenius*. Nicknamed *Myfanwy* ("My Beloved"), the 30,000-year-old remains are now at the Holyhead Maritime Museum.

At the time of our visit, two large oil rigs occupied the docks, one almost blocking our departure.

Holy Isle is dominated by Holyhead Mountain, a rocky quartzite dome, which, at 722 feet, is the highest point on Anglesey, otherwise generally low-lying and fertile. The contrast between Anglesey and nearby and Snowdonia, visible in the distance, is quite dramatic.

Our first visit was to the South Stack RSPB Reserve, only a short coach ride from the ferry terminal, to which we had cruised overnight. Unfortunately, the Visitors' Centre was closed but there was plenty to see, nonetheless.

I joined archaeologist Phoebe Olsen's group at the *Tŷ Mawr* Iron Age stone house settlement. There are now only twenty structures but when first discovered, some fifty years ago, there were over fifty. There is a variety of designs, and it is believed that they would not all have been in use at the same time or for the same purpose – dwellings, storerooms, and animal shelters.

Roman remains have also been found here.

I decided not to join Kevin Morgan's group of eager birdwatchers, exploring the steep and treacherous-looking cliffs. Some of the rocks here predate the Cambrian era, which began 570 million years ago. Instead, I made my own way along the clifftop as far as Elin's Tower, all the while looking out for choughs, one of the main species of interest here.

A member of the crow family, the chough is distinguished by its red beak and legs.

Elin's Tower is a Victorian folly, originally used as a summer house by the notable Stanley family from Penrhos. It is named after Elin, the Welsh wife of the 19th-century politician, William Owen Stanley. It is now (or will again be, post-Covid) used as an RSPB observatory.

From there I headed to South Stack, an islet, 135 feet high and covering no more than 20 acres. The lighthouse complex atop it covers seven acres. Built by Trinity House in 1809, the 91-foot-tall lighthouse is now operated remotely. Prior to 1828, the only access to the lighthouse was in a basket suspended on a hemp cable. Then an iron suspension bridge was built; in 1983 it was replaced by the present aluminium bridge and the lighthouse was opened to the public.

Unfortunately, the lighthouse, like the visitor centre, was Covid-closed and I could get no further than the gate before the bridge.

There are four hundred and eight steps from the bridge to the car park at the top. I know - I counted them!

As I reached the top, a Coastguard Sikorsky S-92A helicopter hovered above the lighthouse before moving further along the coast.

Quite coincidently, I noted a report sometime later that, five days after our visit, a man had been taken to hospital after being winched from the sea off South Stack. Clearly, it is a dangerous stretch of coastline.

After lunch on board, we headed to Plas Cadnant Hidden Gardens, where we were greeted on arrival by the owner, Anthony Taverner.

Situated near the Menai Strait and its iconic bridges and reckoned to be one of the finest gardens in Wales, Plas Cadnant began as a farm in the 16th century.

By the Victorian era, it had become a country estate but deteriorated during the second half of the 20th century until purchased by Taverner. Work started on restoring the gardens and grounds in 1997. It was a huge undertaking as large areas had not been maintained for more than 70 years. Since then, large parts of the gardens have undergone a spectacular transformation and been restored to their former glory.

As we walked into the walled garden, we were welcomed by the gentle sound of the harp being played by an elderly gentleman. What a pleasant and unexpected welcome!

The formal gardens were very beautiful, but I was much more impressed by the informal gardens with paths leading down through trees (and an enormous variety of plants) to the small brook at the bottom.

There I spotted a pair of grey wagtails – and waited in vain for a hoped-for appearance of a dipper. A small robin busied itself amongst the stones on the river floor.

There are also red squirrels here but, sadly, saw I none!

With time to spare, I walked round the "red route" again and it was quieter this time. I was reminded of the song about New York being – "so good I (did) it twice"!

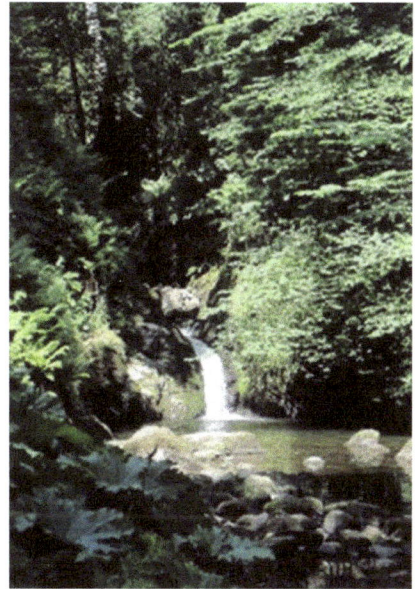

We returned to Holyhead via the south coast of Anglesey, passing near to RAF Valley where, our guide Lynn reminded us, Prince William was based for four years. She regaled us with a few, all homely, stories about his and Kate's stay here.

RAF Valley is a training base for Hawks, and the Red Arrows frequently train here.

Day 8: Fishguard, St David's, Porthclais, the Pembrokeshire Coastal Path, Ramsay and Skomer Islands, and Grassholm

Fishguard sits to the north of the Pembrokeshire peninsula; its name has nothing to do with protection of marine life but is Nordic for "safe harbour". It has been the location for a number of well-known films, such as Burton and Taylor's Under Milk Wood (1971).

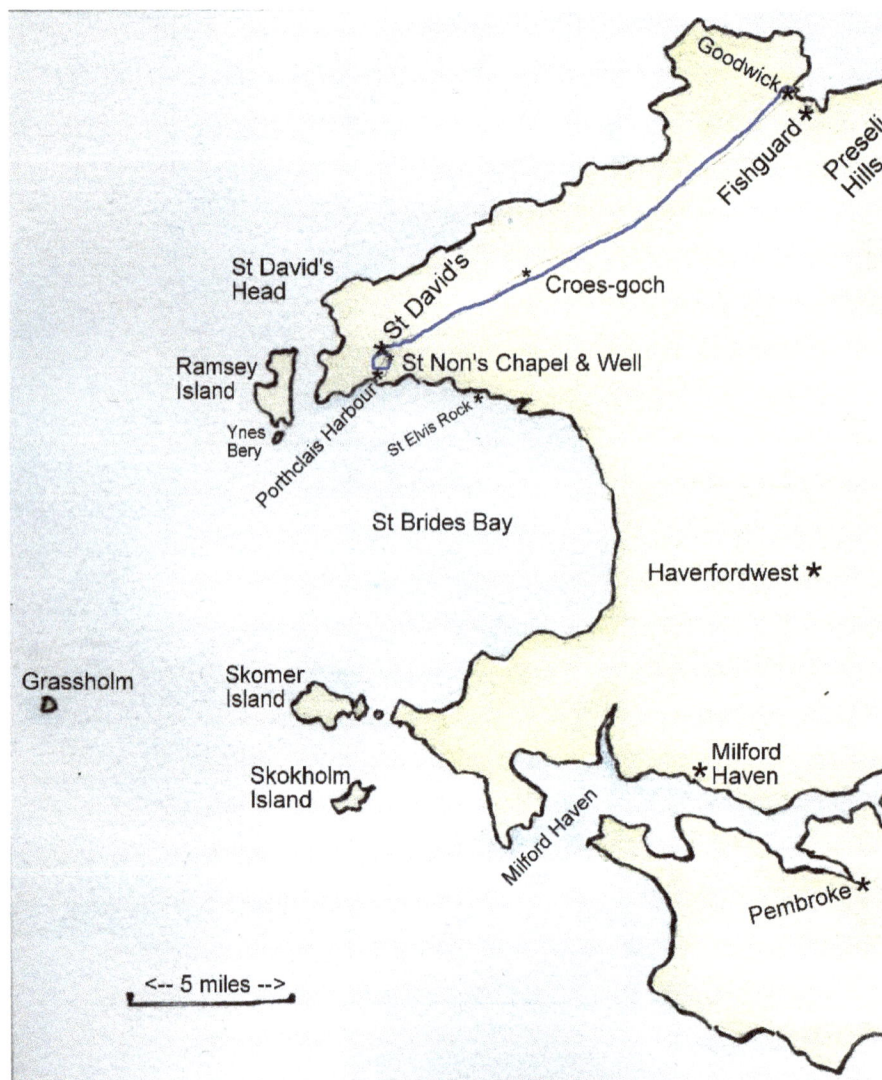

The Battle of Fishguard was the last invasion on British soil and, so the story goes, a French naval boat surrendered to a group of women in February 1797. More credibly, the French forces who had landed mistook as infantry the red coats and shako of local women, gathered on the cliff to watch the forthcoming battle. (But it's a lovely story!)

We had docked across the harbour at Goodwick, from where we could see the Preseli Mountains behind the town. The Preseli Mountains (or Hills – they rise out of the landscape to 1,750 feet) are now famous as the source of the blue dolerite stones used at Stonehenge, 140 miles away.

Our morning trip took us to St David's, well known as the smallest city in the country. We travelled southwest along the A407, the line of the pilgrim's walking route to the cathedral.

(A 12th-century pope had decreed that two trips to St David's were equivalent to one to Rome!)

We paused briefly, as we passed through Croes-goch, at the ancient stone marking the place, about a day's walk from St David's, where pilgrims would meet to share bread (or measure the size of loaf they were allowed to take, according to our guide, David).

Strictly speaking, St David's is the UK's smallest city by population (just over 1,600 in 2011) but the smallest city by local authority boundary area is the City of London!

City status was withdrawn from St David's in 1886 but was restored in 1994 at the request of Queen Elizabeth II.

Although St David – the only one of our four patron saints to be indigenous – lived in the sixth century, the cathedral of St David's is mainly 12th century.

Nearby, are the ruins of the once-upon-a-time magnificent, medieval Bishop's Palace.

Time did not permit a visit to the palace and only a brief look inside the cathedral.

From St David's, about twelve of us walked to Porthclais, an attractive small port where the stone for the cathedral was believed to have landed. Built in the 12th century to import coal and timber, it is now used by local fishermen and recreational sailors. Sadly, the rainy conditions did not little to enhance its fame as a beautiful location.

From there, our bedraggled group walked along a couple of the one hundred and eighty-six miles of the Pembrokeshire Coastal Path. The Pembrokeshire National Park is the only coastal national park in the country.

The weather was not benign and the wild life seemed to be taking refuge, but we did see a pair of ravens and a whitethroat.

A few miles to the east, beyond our walk at the mouth of the River Solva, there is a small rock known as St Elvis Rock. It is not difficult to see the connection in people's minds between that and the Preseli Hills!

On our way we met a group of young people about to begin a coasteering adventure. Rather them than me!

To the west along the coast, we could just make out *Ynes Bery*, a small island at the south end of Ramsay Island.

Turning inland, we stopped at the ruins of St Non's Chapel. St Non was St David's mother and it is believed that St David was born here in 500AD.

Nearby is a well, said to have sprung up when St David was born.

There is a reconstruction of the church a little way off. We did not deem it particularly worthy of a visit.

On our return journey, our guide treated us to a fine rendition of "*Calon Lân*" (Welsh for 'A Pure Heart'). Written in the 1890s by Daniel James and sung to a tune by John Hughes, it was originally written as a hymn, but has become firmly established as a rugby anthem.

I was joined for lunch by Brenda before returning to my cabin to write, while we headed for our next place of interest.

Just off St David's Head, the westernmost point of mainland Wales, lies Ramsay Island and a group of savage-looking rocks. Although less than two miles long and with a highest point only 446 feet above sea level, Ramsay Island is the fourth largest island in Wales. Now a nature reserve, owned and protected by the RSPB, it is home to some thirty species of bird. Finally free of rats and mice, ground- and burrow-nesting birds can breed here safely. A little to the west of Ramsay, on a rocky outcrop, is the South Bishop lighthouse.

From there we sailed to Skomer. Two miles long by 1½ miles wide, it has an area of 720 acres. Most of the island is around 200 feet, with its highest point (Gorse Hill) only 259 feet, above sea level. The name derives from the Viking *Skalmey*, meaning "cleft island", possibly because the eastern end of the island is nearly cut off from the main part.

Skomer is especially well known for its puffins, yet there is so much more to this bird paradise including Manx shearwaters (120,000), dolphins, harbour porpoises, Atlantic grey seal, razorbills, gannets, fulmars and the unique Skomer vole. The island is surrounded by some of the richest waters for wildlife off the British Isles from delightfully coloured sea slugs to magnificent cetaceans.

For environmental reasons, we were not allowed to anchor off Skomer but had to drift, with occasional corrections of position. Inevitably, this might have led to a slower deployment of the Zodiacs but it was not noticeable.

I toured around, with birder Kevin Morgan, viewing amongst others: oystercatcher (above left), buzzard (above right), fulmar (below left), grey seal (below right) and one of the many puffin colonies (bottom).

Harbour porpoises appeared very briefly – too briefly to be photographed. Unsurprisingly, we saw no sign of any of the 20,000 Skomer voles that live here!

After Skomer, we headed out to view the nearby, slightly smaller (twenty-two acres) island of Grassholm and its vast gannet colony.

A small uninhabited island, lying about seven miles to the west of Skomer, it is the westernmost point in Wales other than the isolated rocks on which the Smalls Lighthouse stands. The gannet colony is so extensive that, in the breeding season, half of the island looks white, half green.

Day 9: Lundy Island

I awoke around 6:50 as our ship rounded the north end of Lundy. It was raining! The warm, dry, sunny conditions of the Outer Hebrides seemed to be well behind us now, although the weather did improve as the day progressed.

Lying in the Bristol Channel, about ten miles off the North Devon coast, Lundy is about three miles long and five-eighths of a mile wide and measures about 1,100 acres. It is largely composed of 55/60-million-year-old granite, rather younger than Devon and Cornwall and, unlike them, heavily glaciated. Beacon Hill, at the north end of the island is its highest point (469 feet).

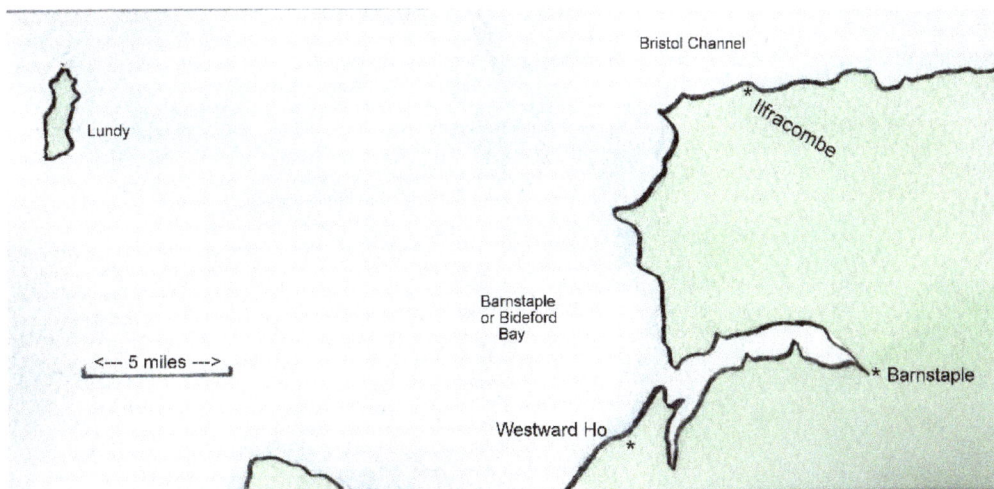

In Norse, '*Lundy*' means 'Puffin Island' – no surprise to young philatelists of my generation who knew it for its locally-issued stamps, value half and one puffin, first-and-only printed on November 1, 1929.

Although the British Government considered that the Puffin stamps were not actual postal duty, in fact no letter can now leave Lundy without Puffinage being applied and modern Lundy stamps are legal postage in the United Kingdom.

The (only) post-box on Lundy is painted blue rather than the normal red.

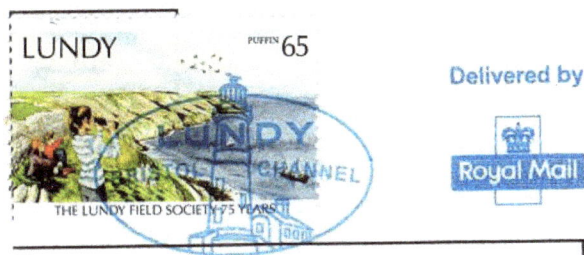

In the 1920s, self-proclaimed king, Martin Harman, not satisfied with stamps alone, tried to issue his own coinage and was fined by the House of Lords. With a long history of changing ownership, Lundy was purchased in 1969 by British millionaire Jack Hayward, who donated it to the National Trust. It is now managed by the Landmark Trust.

There are about twenty-eight permanent inhabitants and an increasing number of rental cottages plus camping facilities that help the island's finances.

The 1958 German-built MS Oldenburg sails at least three times a week from either Bideford or Ilfracombe, according to tides, and the crossing takes about 2 hours each way.

There is also a helicopter service and there is a small grass runway, which, unfortunately, I failed to notice until it was too late to investigate it fully.

The ship anchored in the appropriately-named Landing Bay near the only spot where it is possible to land! We were transported to the island by Zodiac with a (slightly) wet landing, ably aided by the expedition team.

Phil, naturalist Michelle Sole, nine others and I set off on a walk around (most of) the island.

On the way up the narrow track from the harbour, we noted a small herd of wild goats on the steep hillside.

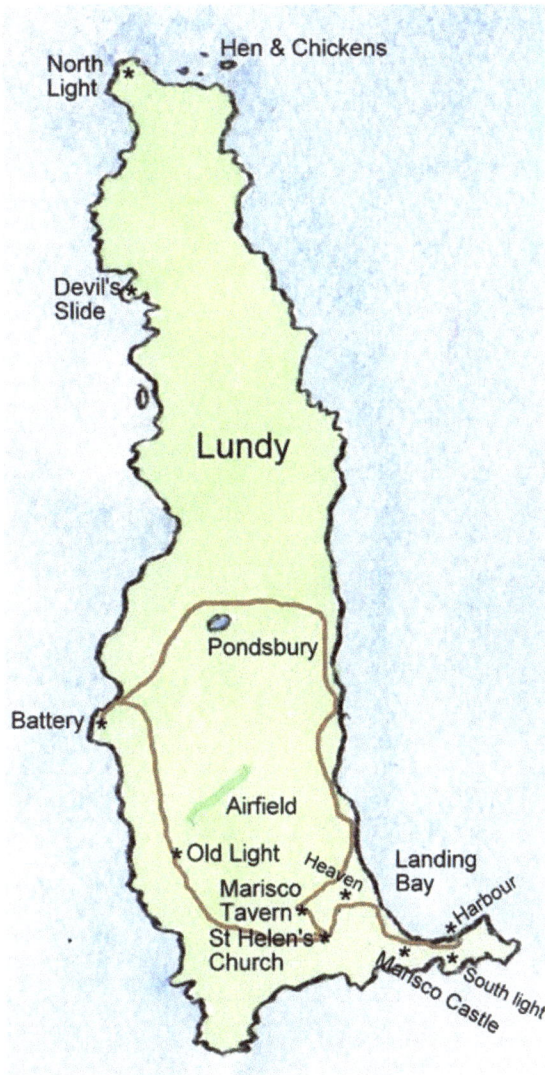

A little further on we saw the idyllically placed house, former home of the Heaven family who owned Lundy until 1917.

Not surprisingly, the locals would refer to Lundy as the Kingdom of Heaven. (One of our party suggested that the steep path up to the house was, therefore, the Stairway to Heaven!)

Life wasn't all sublime for the family, however; Heaven went bankrupt building the church and the track down to the harbour.

From the cliff top, we headed southwards to the "Pirate's Castle". Pirates who terrorised this coast, the de Marisco family held Lundy from the twelfth century to 1321.

As reputed descendants of a royal bastard, they made claims to the throne. Marisco Castle was built in 1243 after Henry III had executed William de Marisco for treason.

The Keep is approximately square in plan with projecting towers on the east and west sides. Fishermen's cottages were built around the mid-19th century; they were remodelled again as holiday cottages by the Landmark Trust in the late 20th century.

From the castle, we headed up the west coast towards the old lighthouse.

Built in the 1820s on the rocky summit of Chapel Hill, the granite tower was 96 feet high with the keepers' houses adjoining. In an innovative experiment, two lights were shone from the tower, a lower fixed white light and an upper white light flashing every 60 seconds.

However, the light revolved so quickly that no period of darkness was detectable between the flashes so in effect this also appeared as a fixed light. This appearance of being a fixed light contributed to a disaster on one evening in November 1828. In thick fog, *La Jeune Emma*, travelling from Martinique to Cherbourg, mistook the Lundy lights for the fixed light of Ushant (a French island some two hundred miles away) and went onto the rocks. Of the nineteen people on board, thirteen were lost, including a niece of the Empress Josephine. Following this, Trinity House built two new lighthouses on the North and South extremities of the island in 1897 and discontinued the old often-fog-obscured lighthouse.

Today, the lighthouse cottages are available for holiday rental and the lighthouse itself is open to visitors. There are one hundred and forty-seven steps to the top, from where there are fine views of the island.

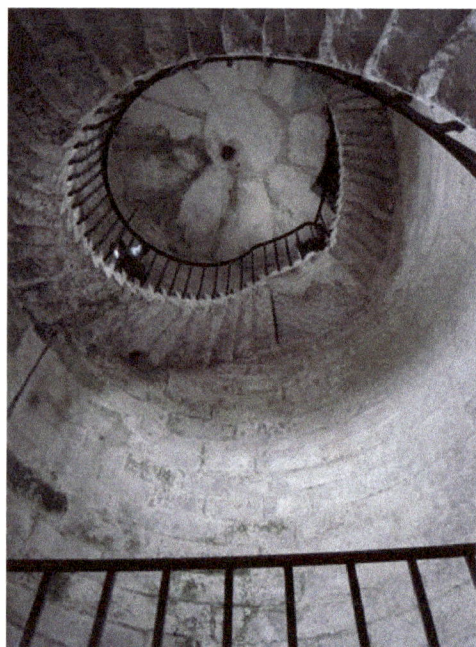

We continued up the west coast towards the battery, built in 1863 at the westernmost point to warn ships. A cannon was fired every ten minutes in times of fog.

The ruggedness of the western cliffs was evident here. Surprisingly, a small group of botanists was on the slopes gathering (or recording) plants.

From here, we headed across the island and caught sight of several Soay sheep – possibly the second most important flock worldwide. Soay sheep were introduced from St. Kilda to Lundy by Martin Coles Harman soon after he purchased the island in 1925. The Soay sheep is physically similar to the wild ancestors of domestic sheep, the Mediterranean mouflon and the horned urial sheep of Central Asia.

Approaching Pondsbury, the largest of the ponds constructed on Lundy to store water during the often-dry summers, we were fortunate to come across a fine example of a Lundy pony. The breed originated in 1928, when Harman introduced thirty-four New Forest pony mares, eight foals, and a Welsh Mountain B strawberry roan stallion. It was quite unperturbed by our passing.

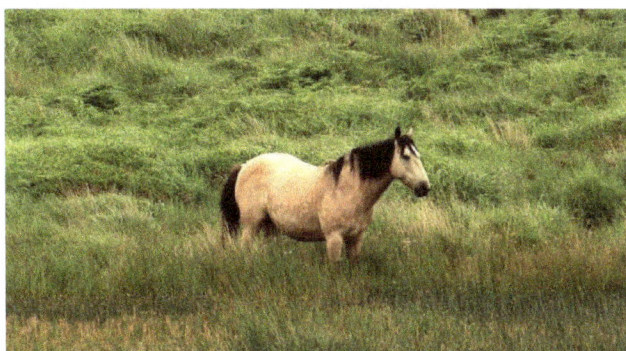

The ponies bred very successfully – too successfully! – and in 1980, the National Trust moved the entire herd to Cornwall. Later, however, the Lundy Pony Society brought back some of the mares and foals.

Beyond the pond, the path disappeared as we walked eastwards and for a few yards we got, literally, bogged down.

Although he had chanced upon it on a previous visit, Phil was unable to find the wreckage of one of the two Heinkel He 111 bombers that crash landed on the island in 1941.

As we walked, we spotted, amongst other birds, wheatears, stonechats, larks, linnets and ravens (one a bit moth-eaten) as well as the usual sea bird colonies. (I learned that the wheatear was originally known as the white-arse, for obvious reasons. I thought you would probably want to know that.)

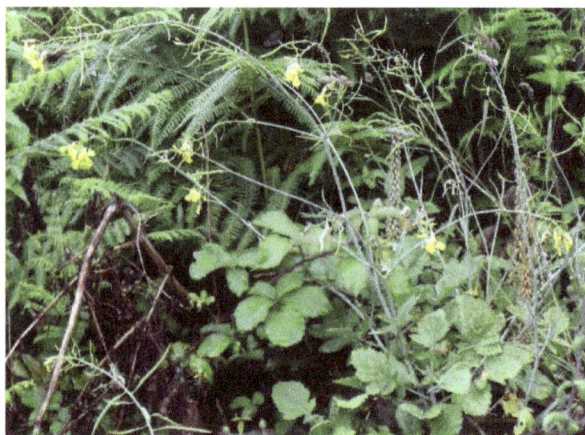

We also saw some examples of Lundy cabbage (*Coincya wrightii*, for the classicists), a species of primitive brassica, endemic to the island of Lundy, where it is sufficiently isolated to have formed its own species. (It did not look particularly appetising!)

At one time, there was a quarry at the north end of the island. Some ruins of quarry buildings, a hospital and cottages built for the workers still remain.

On our way south along the eastern path, we met and chatted to a very nice, middle-aged couple who were camping. They told us that they had been awakened about two o'clock in the morning by the sound of the Manx shearwaters returning to their nests. (Until a decade ago there were just a few hundred pairs left on the island and their eggs and chicks were being eaten by rats. The Seabird Recovery Project partnership was formed to save them by removing the rats. There are now 5-5,500 breeding pairs of shearwaters on Lundy.)

We ended our tour of the island at the Marisco Tavern, Lundy's only pub. It is the pub that never shuts - although alcohol is only served during permitted hours - and it is the only building on the island to have lighting after the generators shut down for the night.

While some of my co-passengers stopped for a well-deserved beer, I headed for the shop to buy postcards and, of course, Lundy stamps. (I was given an extra stamp, with margin impression (see illustration), because I had bought so many and had said that I collected stamps.)

By the time I had written and posted cards, everyone else had disappeared back to the harbour and for a moment I was uncertain of the way back. We had been told that St Helen's Church was not open to visitors because they were preparing it for the wedding of a local couple that afternoon.

It seemed to be in the right direction, and when I saw someone going in, I followed to ask directions. But despite calling out, I received no response. In the event, I did find my way back in time for the last Zodiac to the ship – and got a sneaky shot inside the church into the bargain!

Over lunch, back on board, Brenda and Chef Tracie came across to chat.

After lunch we enjoyed a talk by Phil on the Barbary slaves and the true meaning of the words of Rule Britannia – an exhortation to Britannia to rule, not a declaration that it does already rule, the waves.

We cruised around the east, north and west sides of the island with a flow of snippets of information over the loudspeaker system from Sue.

At north end, we could see the northern lighthouse. There are some small skerries here, known as the Hen and Chickens. Sue also pointed out a fracture in the crust and a lava-filled dyke.

On the west coast, we spotted climbers (circled, below) on the Devil's Slide. First climbed in the early 1960s, the 380-foot face has been claimed to be the tallest granite slab in Europe.

A little further south we had a view of the battery and the steep staircase that we had climbed earlier. The wall is known as the three-quarter wall; there is also a half-wall and a quarter-wall that divide the island east-to-west.)

From here, we headed for the Isles of Scilly, one hundred and twenty miles away to the southwest.

I enjoyed a pleasant dinner with Brenda, and Elizabeth and John (farmers from south of Catterick). Afterwards, we moved to the Club, where we were joined by Phil. Brenda, Phil and I enjoyed several Glenmorangies (until they ran out!). Elizabeth and John did not drink but seemed happy enough just to chat.

All in all, a most enjoyable and informative day and a very pleasant evening.

Day 10: Isles of Scilly – Tresco and St Mary's

Most people will think of the Isles of Scilly as being hot and sunny, warmed by the waters of the Gulf Stream. I will remember them also as being wet and windswept!

An archipelago of five inhabited and one hundred and forty other islands off the Cornish coast, the Isles of Scilly cover an area of just over six square miles (just over 4,000 acres). The total population is about two thousand two hundred.

The main islands are St Mary's, Tresco, St Martin's, Bryher and St Agnes. They are covered in heathland and fringed by sandy beaches. Low-lying, the highest point at only 167 feet above sea level, is Telegraph on St Mary's.

The isles were designated as a World Heritage Site in 2001

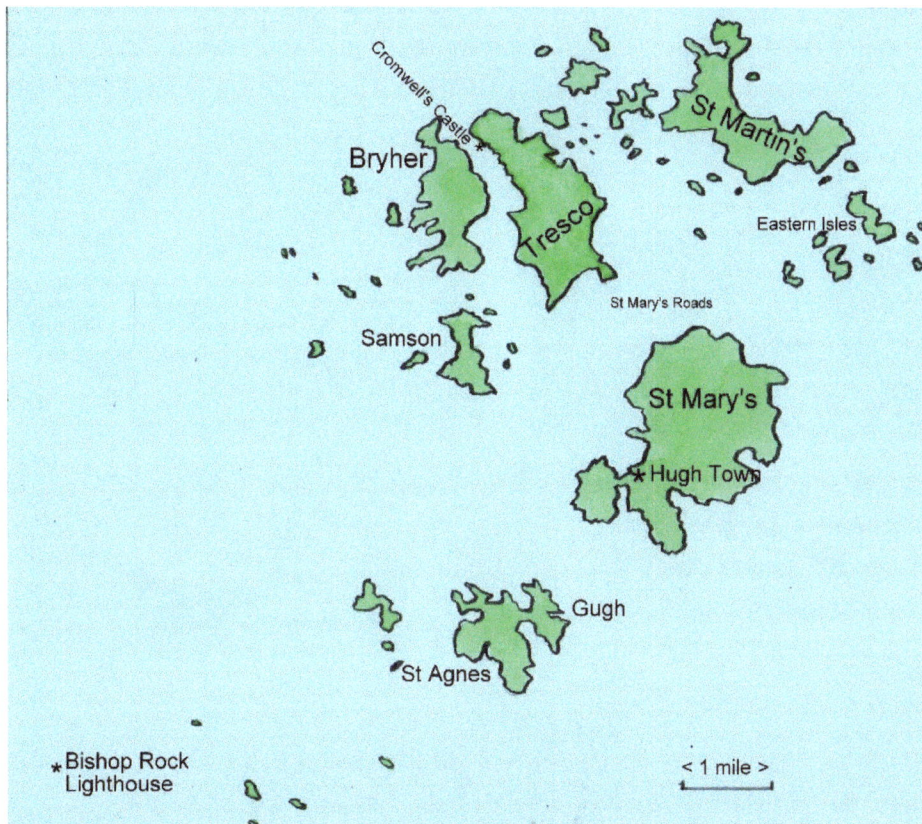

We arrived at our anchorage in St Mary's Roads (between St Mary's and Tresco) just a little before 8 a.m., after a fairly choppy voyage from Lundy. It was calm in the shelter of the islands, however.

Landing on Tresco required us all to undergo another lateral flow test for Covid-19. Fortunately, but not unexpectedly, we all proved negative.

The five-minute Zodiac trip took us to Cairn Near at the southernmost tip of the island. From there, it is only a short walk to Tresco Abbey Gardens. On the way, we passed the terminal buildings, and crossed the very short grass runway, of Tresco Heliport.

There are regular flights, operated by Penzance Helicopters between Penzance and Tresco and St Mary's. Two helicopters – one privately owned, probably an Agusta A109, and the other an AgustaWestland AW139 operated by Castle Air Charters - landed and took off.

I also spotted, across the water, the Isles of Scilly Skybus De Havilland Canada DHC-6-300 Twin Otter taking off from St Mary's on its flight to Land's End (20 minutes), Newquay (30 minutes) or Exeter (one hour).

Augustus Smith purchased the Isles of Scilly from the Duchy of Cornwall. At the time "no corner of Great Britain stood in greater need of help than Scilly".

He began the creation of Tresco Abbey Gardens in 1834, around the ruins of the Benedictine Abbey. With the help of Scillonian master mariners, he established an extraordinary collection of over four thousand different plant species from around the world.

He laid out the gardens around the 12th century St Nicholas Priory. There are zones according to the source of the plants – "Higher and Lower Australia", "Mexico", "South Africa Cliff" and so on.

There are also ancient and modern artworks interspersed along the paths.

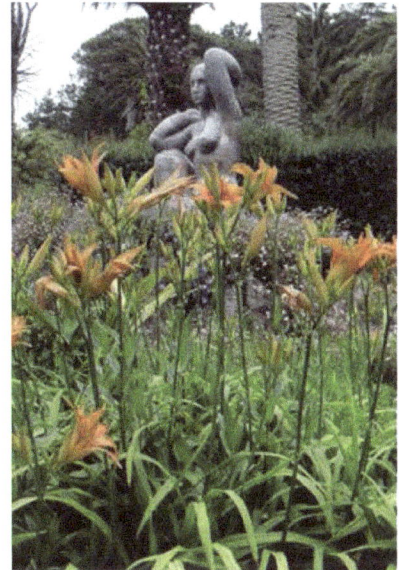

We saw red squirrels feeding boldly, within almost touching distance, as well as golden pheasants.

Within the gardens is the Valhalla Museum, a collection of figureheads from ships wrecked on the rocks surrounding the Isles of Scilly.

After my visit to the gardens, I walked around the southern half of the island on a narrow but well-built roadway towards New Grimsby (quite different to the "old" Grimsby I once knew).

I left the road to walk up to the monument to Lieutenant Thomas Algernon Smith-Dorrien-Smith JP DL, who succeeded his uncle, Augustus Smith, as Proprietor of the Isles of Scilly in 1872, and continued the development of the Tresco Abbey Gardens.

The spot affords an excellent view of the southern islands.

I descended from there and continued my walk along the beautiful, sandy Apple Tree Bay (no sign of an apple tree) to the pier for the return Zodiac.

After lunch, our planned destination became St Mary's. Our planned afternoon trip to Bryher Island had to be postponed because of the extremely poor weather.

The prospect of a wet afternoon spent wandering around St Mary's did not actually appeal but, as I had never visited the island before and it seemed a better alternative to spending the afternoon on board ship, off I went.

The authorities did not allow us to use Zodiacs to visit St Mary's but instead we had to transfer from the Island Sky to a tender. Twenty-two hardy souls (and some a lot more "foolhardy" than "hardy") ventured aboard the tender, Sapphire.

The swell made boarding quite difficult, and we were advised that, on our return, we might have to be taken to Tresco by tender and then brought to the ship by Zodiac.

It rained all the way to St Mary's, all the time we were there, and all the way back! There is not a lot to do in Hugh Town, the main population centre of St Mary's, on a dreich afternoon. The joys of a British summer!

St Mary's is the largest island of this archipelago. Its capital (i.e. only town), Hugh Town, is a pleasant enough little settlement, and I have no doubt that it would be enjoyable to visit on a fine day. The weather being as it was, however, I did not linger but walked briskly through it to the RNLI station where there was a small shop.

There, I chatted with the elderly lady. Her son was a lifeguard but, a few years ago, he had had one leg amputated in a rescue mission. Her two grandsons are also RNLI volunteers. What spirit!

She asked if I had seen Wally, the walrus that has been frequenting the islands and causing havoc by clambering onto small boats. It has become quite a celebrity! All of her family except her have seen it. Needless to say, I had not - and never did.

Estimated to weigh in at around 1,800 lb, Wally left Scilly and swam to County Cork. Three weeks after leaving Ireland, in September, he was spotted in Iceland.

I bought a pair of port (red) and starboard (green) socks and put a donation in the tin. A few others arrived from the ship so, hopefully, her afternoon will have been deemed a success.

On the advice of Phoebe, whom I chanced to meet, I walked out to see the antique guns at King Charles's battery. The battery was built in the 1740s to replace an earlier one and defends the entrance to the harbour from St Mary's Sound.

Most of the guns date from around 1800, but one was cast (and numbered) at Carron Ironworks, Falkirk, in 1812.

Next, I walked up the hill to the garrison, now the Star Castle Hotel.

Built in 1593 following the Spanish Armada of 1588, the garrison is in the shape of an eight-pointed star that features on the flag of the Council of the Isles of Scilly.

Strategically placed gun batteries at regular intervals around the outer wall, allowed covering fire at all angles.

The Scillonian III, the regular ferry between St Mary's and the mainland, was docked at St Mary's as we left. It has a relatively flat bottom so that it can navigate the shallow waters around the islands and, as a result, is notorious for its bumpy rides in rough seas. She is one of only three ships in the world still carrying the status of Royal Mail Ship.

The wind had got up a bit more on our return journey, but we were able to transfer from the tender direct to the ship.

I dined again with Elizabeth and John then we went up to the Club and sat with Peter and Alison. I resolutely declined the Glenmorangie! Both couples have travelled extensively, all round the world - no kidding!

Day 11: Isles of Scilly – Bryher, St Agnes and Gugh

After a fairly turbulent night, despite being in the lee of St Mary's, where the ship had repositioned overnight, I awoke to sunshine and a complete absence of rain. Joy!

Our trip to Bryher had to be by tender but, on this occasion, because of the choppy conditions, the captain of the tender would not tie up behind the Island Sky. And so, we were obliged to transfer from ship to Zodiac and Zodiac to tender.

Bryher runs parallel to and to the west of Tresco. It is about four miles from where we were anchored to the northeast of St Mary's, and it took about an hour to get there.

The island has a length of 1.2 miles, a maximum width of 0.6 miles and covers an area of 330 acres. There are about ninety residents.

From our landing spot, we could see Cromwell's Castle on Tresco, across the narrow (200 yard) Tresco Channel. On a very low spring tide, it is possible to walk between Tresco and Bryher.

Built following the Parliamentary invasion of the Isles of Scilly in 1651, it comprises a tall, circular gun tower and an adjacent gun platform, and was designed to prevent enemy naval vessels from entering the harbour. It is one of the few surviving Cromwellian fortifications in Britain.

With only one hour to explore, I headed south-west across the island, passing the island shop on the way.

Bryher was exactly what I had expected of one of the isles of Scilly – sunny, warm with beautifully tended gardens and small, quiet lanes devoid of all traffic except the occasional small, all-terrain vehicle.

The view looking west across Hell Bay towards the wide-open Atlantic was stunning.

Wandering off track at one point, I was excited at the thought that I had spotted some redpolls. I was assured, later, by Kevin that what I had seen were linnets. Lovely little birds, nonetheless! Like so many of our songbirds, linnet numbers have dropped substantially over the past few decades, with the UK population estimated to have declined by 57 per cent between 1970 and 2014.

All of our party were assembled at the pier in good time for our return to the ship. It was announced that an official from the harbourmaster's office was on his way to check our boarding passes! Really! We had to wait for half-an-hour under a now-blazing sun. What a lot of nonsense! I shall now refer to them, not as their preferred Isles of Scilly, but as The Scilly Isles.

Dressed for the anticipated foul weather, I was obliged, on the trip back, to fashion a hat out of a life-vest bag to protect my head from the blazing sun. Not a good look – but very effective!

After a quick lunch, when I was joined by Brenda, it was time to head out again, this time for St Agnes. Again, the process was Zodiac to tender, tender to island.

It was a long haul from ship to St Agnes and at times the sea was quite choppy.

The name of the island derives, not from some pious nun or miracle-maker of old, but from the Cornish ek-enys meaning "far-off island". The island's apparent beatification is much more recent!

St Agnes is the south-westernmost of the inhabited islands. Together with adjoining Gugh, it is about one mile across and stretches to just 366 acres, and hosts about eighty-five inhabitants.

About five miles beyond St Agnes, on a tiny skerry, is the 161-foot-high Bishop Rock Lighthouse, constructed in 1858. (The original iron lighthouse was begun in 1847 but was washed away before it could be completed.)

I opted to walk with Phil and Kevin's group, and we headed southwest. Our walk took us past Big Pool, across which we could see the St. Agnes lighthouse. Built in 1680, it was only the second lighthouse station to be established by Trinity House.

Big Pool is one of only two freshwater pools on the island. It is a Site of Special Scientific Interest and is described it as a "mesotrophic freshwater habitat". Well, there you go! As the poet John Pomfret said, some three hundred and thirty years ago, with amazing insight, "we live and learn but not the wiser grow".

We stopped at Troytown Farm for ice cream. Not having eaten for all of two hours, I had the lemon meringue flavour with a dollop of clotted cream on top! Absolutely delicious!

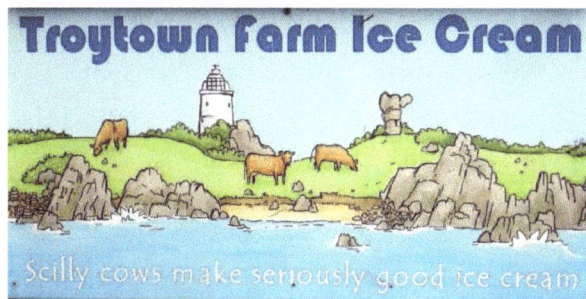

We passed by the so-called "Troytown Maze", a pebble maze thought to be of medieval origin. The edges of the routes are made up of stones half buried in the ground. The maze is unicursal; that is, it does not contain dead ends, as in a puzzle maze, but comprises a single path which leads inevitably to the centre.

It reminded me of the labyrinth at St Columba's Bay, Iona. Both equally quite underwhelming!

There are many weird and wonderful rock formations on the island of St Agnes. The Nag's Head is probably the most remarkable. Standing at around 15 feet tall, it has an appendage that looks rather like an old horse's head - hence the name.

Heading back towards the pier, I took a small detour to walk across the tombola (sandbar) to the island of Gugh (pronounced as in Hugh). Only about ½ mile long, about 1/3 mile wide, and covering 90 acres, Gugh could arguably be described as the sixth inhabited island in the Scilly archipelago but is usually included with St Agnes.

I learned two new words on this trip – "tombola" from the Italian *tombolo*, meaning "pillow" and "tarbert", literally meaning "boat-carrying", which appear to apply more-or-less to the same physical feature of an isthmus!

All safely on board, we returned, unscathed, to the ship, with much happier memories of the Scilly Isles.

After the daily "recap", there was an auction for an illustrated map of our cruise by Ian Bullock. I won, paying far more than the limit I had set myself at the start, but happy to have done so. It is illustrated at the beginning and on the cover of this book.

Justin joined John, Elizabeth, and me for dinner, after which we retired to the Club and enjoyed a few Glenlivets and the company of four other couples.

Day 12: Fowey

Overnight, we sailed the eighty-or-so miles from the Scilly Isles towards South Cornwall.

I awoke just before seven o'clock as the MS Island Sky manoeuvred into its anchorage in the River Fowey, opposite the town of Fowey (pronounced "Foy").

The town, population about two thousand three hundred, has been in existence since well before the Norman invasion. The estuary of the River Fowey forms a natural harbour and has been a significant international trading port since the medieval period. It is still a working port today.

We had to transfer from ship to land via Zodiacs.

With nine other passengers, I joined Phil and Kevin on the four-mile Hall Walk from Bodinnick to Polruan. The footpath dates from at least the 16th century and was created by the Mohun family of nearby Hall.

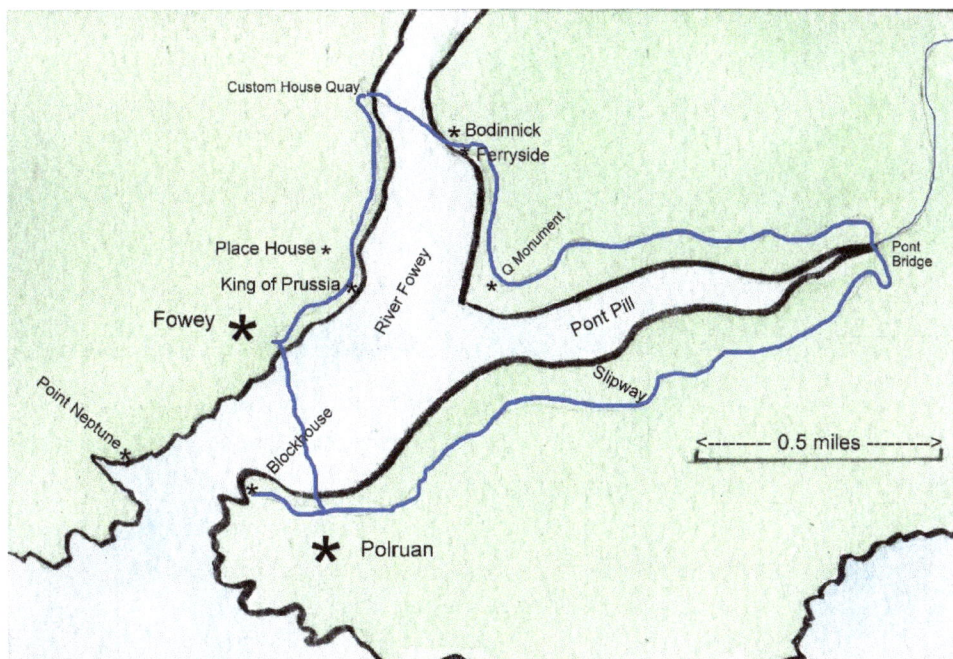

The walk is said to provide unparalleled views of the harbour and I cannot dispute that, although the weather – almost constant rain - was hardly conducive to a stroll through the forest. Off we went, nevertheless, wandering at first through the Old Town, before we crossed the river by the car ferry to Bodinnick. There has been a ferry here since the 13th century.

It is a steep climb from the ferry at Bodinnick. At the top of the hill, we took the path that led downriver on the eastern bank.

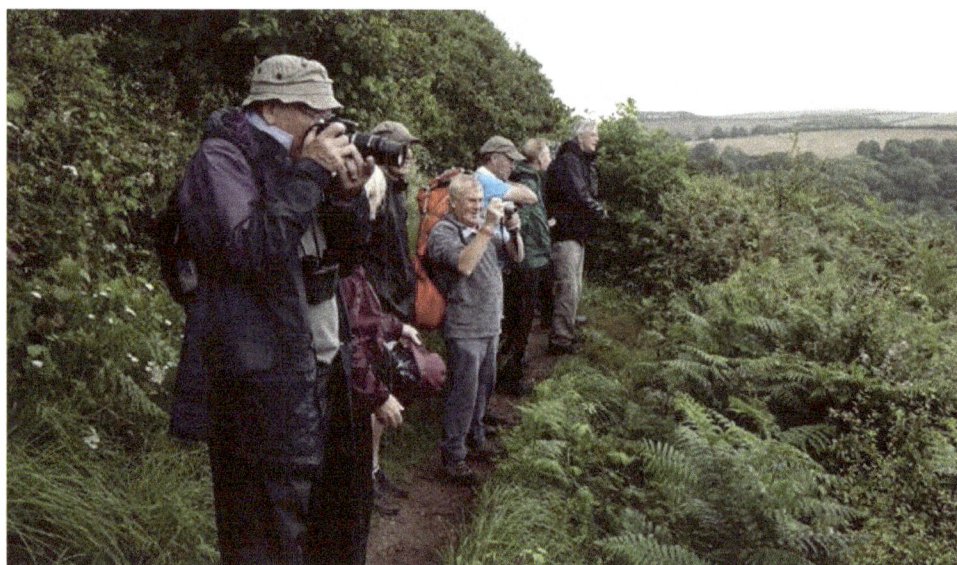

Phil pointed out Place House, on the other side, in the heart of Fowey. Since the 13th century, it has been the home of the Treffry family, wealthy merchants exporting tin, fish and wool. In 1475, so the story goes, Dame Elizabeth, whose husband was away fighting in France, rallied her household and successfully repelled French marauders, who had destroyed the church, by pouring boiling lead, stripped from the roof, upon the heads of the attackers.

A little later, we stopped at the Q Memorial. Sir Arthur Thomas Quiller-Couch was a Cornish writer who published under the pseudonym Q. Although a prolific novelist, he is remembered mainly for the monumental publication "The Oxford Book of English Verse" 1250–1900 and for his literary criticism.

After Quiller-Couch died in 1944, his novel about Tristan and Iseult was discovered, unfinished, amongst his papers. It seems entirely appropriate that an author of the calibre of Daphne Du Maurier, with her Fowey connections, should have been chosen to complete "Castle Dor".

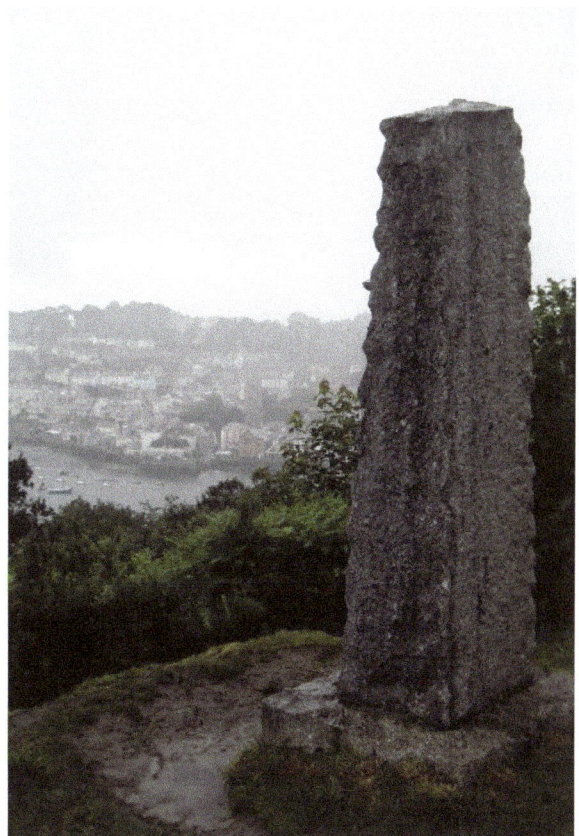

From there, the path turns eastwards along the banks of Pont Pill. At this point, we were afforded what would have been a spectacular view of Polruan and the river estuary - had the weather been somewhat kinder. It was eye-catching, nonetheless.

On the far side of the river, we could just make out the slipway where D-Day landing craft were built.

Fowey became one of the main ports in Cornwall for loading ammunition for the US 29th Division which landed on Omaha Beach. Because of this it was a well-defended town and harbour.

There are many defensive remnants around the area, one of which (a pillbox) we passed on our way.

Over one thousand American troops were based in Fowey prior to embarking for France in the June 1944.

Avoiding the use of a rather hazardous looking Cornish style, we descended and crossed the river at Pont Bridge, noted the ancient lime kilns, climbed again, and turned westwards, heading to Polruan.

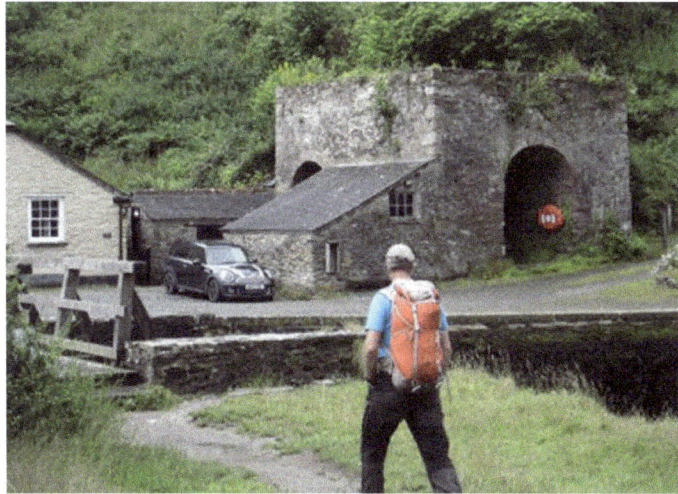

Along the way, some of the more astute birders amongst us – not I, I must confess - identified the calls of a variety of common avian species.

At Polruan, we visited the chain tower, or Polruan Blockhouse, one of only five known to exist in England. It and the chain tower on the opposite bank of the river were built around 1380, the earliest chain towers to have been constructed. A chain was hung between both to prevent undesirable ships entering the harbour.

One of the most complete examples of a chain tower, and little altered since its construction, the Polruan chain tower became obsolete in the 1520s when St Catherine's Castle was built at Fowey. It was, however, reused briefly during the Civil War.

Across the river from the blockhouse can also be seen Point Neptune, a grand 40-bed Italianate mansion. Built in the mid-19th century for William Rashleigh of Menabilly, on the site of an old Napoleonic gun battery that guarded the harbour, it was pointed out to us as the home of Daphne du Maurier. However, my later research has revealed that, in fact, the authoress rented only the former stables and carriage house that had been converted into Point Neptune Cottage, known locally as Readymoney Cottage.

Du Maurier lived there between 1942 and 1943 before moving further west to Menabilly, later immortalised as Manderley in her novel 'Rebecca'.

Point Neptune was sold for £3 million in 2021 by comedian Dawn French, who had bought it with her then-husband, Lenny Henry, in 2006.

A short trip by passenger ferry took us from Polruan right into the centre of Fowey, from where it was a few minutes' walk to the pier and our Zodiacs back to the ship. On the way we passed the "pink house" - The King of Prussia hotel situated in the Town Quay.

It is thought that the establishment was named after John Carter, one of Cornwall's most prodigious smugglers in the 18th century. He was known as the King of Prussia because he supposedly resembled Frederick the Great. Unusually, Carter was a stanch Methodist and his brother, Harry, delivered quayside sermons. No foul language was allowed on board their ships, and he was noted for his good deeds and even his honesty! (One tale is that he broke into a government bond to steal back the pirated tea that the authorities had impounded. He took only his own goods!)

During our walk, some of the other passengers and crew visited the delights of Fowey. Assistant cruise director, Fiona Veal, took the opportunity to savour a Cornish pasty. Perhaps the expedition team were not as well fed as we, the passengers, were!

After lunch, by which time the weather had improved markedly, leisurely Zodiac trips up the Fowey estuary were arranged. I went with Michelle, Brenda, and two fellow passengers.

It is, unquestionably, a beautiful part of the world – despite the unsightly kaolin (china clay) terminal. Fortunately – and probably not by chance – this is hidden from Fowey, round a bend in the river.

Fowey is an important port, and some 450,000 tonnes of cargo are exported each year. This is mainly china clay but other cargoes, such as rock salt and aggregate, are also handled.

Apart from the stunning scenery and attractive riverside properties, we had excellent views of fishing Little Egrets, with their comically unreal black legs and yellow-banana feet….

… and an abundance of black-headed gulls that seemed determined to take over every available roosting spot.

Daphne du Maurier first lived at Ferryside, opposite the town at Bodinnick, before moving to Point Neptune Cottage and then a few miles away to Menabilly. She wrote her first novel, "The Loving Spirit" (1931), at the former boatyard, which had been converted into a holiday home by her parents.

On my return to the ship, I had coffee and a most enjoyable chat with Ian Bullock to decide what to put on the chart that he will prepare for me.

At around six o'clock, we weighed anchor and left Fowey, accompanied by the pilot, to head along the coast to our final destination, Portsmouth.

After dinner we were treated to a showing of film of the whole cruise, put together by Michelle with footage from all the other expedition team members. It was an excellent production and a reminder of the many adventures we had experienced.

The winner of the charity raffle was announced. Excluding my own contributions, total charitable donations amounted to less than £5 per head. Perhaps it confirmed my initial thoughts about some of my fellow passengers.

In discussion with Scots Marilyn and Allan, it transpired that his mother went to Wishaw High School – a good few years before me, of course, but what a coincidence!

I dined enjoyably with Brian and Graham before an early retiral to pack for an early breakfast and even earlier luggage-collection in the morning.

Day 13: Portsmouth and Home

The end of the road or, rather, the cruise!

We approached our final docking at breakfast time, after an uneventful overnight leg. We docked between heavy load carrier Bravewind and Virgin Voyages' Scarlet Lady – two different concepts of the future, perhaps. These are certainly not Natural Wonders, but "wonders" in their own ways, nevertheless.

The fan blades on the former gave some indication of the size of the windfarms that are mushrooming in an effort to save the planet. As always, there are opposing views of the nett effectiveness of such structures – but at least we are trying.

The Scarlet Lady, all seventeen decks of her, dwarfed the MS Island Sky Even looking at the stern, the skyline was dominated by her. There was a general consensus amongst my fellow passengers that this would NOT be their choice vessel for their next, or indeed any, cruise! On this, at least, I heartily concurred.

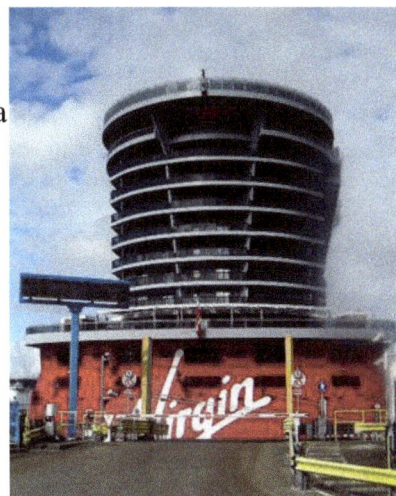

And so, after two short coach rides, I awaited the train from Portsmouth Harbour Station to London and thence home, where I could reflect on a most enjoyable cruise and the sighting of many Natural (and other) Wonders of the British Isles.

THE END

Index

Lightning Source UK Ltd.
Milton Keynes UK
UKHW051141060223
416527UK00007B/175

9 781471 002663